WHAT HAPPENS IN BALI

WHAT HAPPENS IN
BA

Richard Shears

LI

**Drugs, murder and misadventure
from the dark side of the
island paradise**

CONTENTS

	Acknowledgements 7
One	Destiny…Bali 9
Two	A Cocktail of Life 13
Three	The Body in a Suitcase 17
Four	Mick Jagger and Jerry Hall's Balinese Wedding That Never Was 23
Five	Shattered Dreams 29
Six	Gruesome Evidence Laid Out in the Midday Sun . . . 35
Seven	Bali's Other 'Hotel' – Kerobokan Prison 45
Eight	The Breakout 51
Nine	The 'Precious One' and the English Model 59
Ten	Airport Drama – and a Curious Confession 65
Eleven	Casanovas and Schoolies 71

Twelve	'Never, Ever, Take the Balinese for Granted'.	79
Thirteen	'Ganja Queen'.	89
Fourteen	Goodbye to the 'Last Paradise' as the Bombs Explode	97
Fifteen	'007' to the Rescue	113
Sixteen	Death of a Policeman	121
Seventeen	Foreigners and Drugs	133
Eighteen	'A Very Brutal Murder'.	145
Nineteen	Schapelle Freed, but Lindsay Stays on Death Row.	153
Twenty	Bali 'Sex' Life	165
Twenty-One	Dogs and Monkeys	173
Twenty-Two	The Bali Nine.	183
Twenty-Three	They Sang Hymns Before the Rifles Blazed	193
Twenty-Four	The Perils of Bintang	201

ACKNOWLEDGEMENTS

Thank you to *The Jakarta Post, The Bali Times, Jakarta Globe, Bali Post,* News Ltd, *The Sydney Morning Herald,* Australian Broadcasting Corporation, *Brisbane Times, Chicago Tribune* and *Daily Mail.*

I am also grateful for the help of the Indonesian/Balinese lawyers who have been involved in trials, as well as the many Bali-based journalists and photographers who have been of guidance, even if it has only been a 'nod and a wink'.

CHAPTER ONE

DESTINY...BALI

Finally, there was hope. The years had been filled with hatred, deceit, physical pain and misery and she could see no real end to it. But now, on a $10,000 business-class flight across the world, her daughter's eyes closed in the window seat beside her listening to music, wealthy socialite Sheila von Wiese-Mack prayed that the acrimony between her and Heather would melt away in the tropical sunshine that lay ahead. Sheila, 62, had taken her daughter, 19, overseas from their Chicago home before and while at first things had begun to improve each time it wasn't long before the arguments had started again. The problem in recent times had been Heather's boyfriend. Sheila had told Heather numerous times that she just didn't like him. He was black and she insisted he was a fraud – an argument which failed to convince Heather, because her own late father, renowned jazz composer James Mack, had been black.

But this time, as she'd told friends and family members before setting off from their wealthy home in the Oak Park district, Sheila was determined to heal all wounds. Sheila had benefitted from the royalties from her late husband's music but she was determined that Heather, while being raised in a privileged home, would not become a spoilt child with the money that was left following the death of her 76-year-old musician father.

On this holiday, she would ensure that Heather would have the best of everything. A luxury hotel awaited them. There were miles of beaches. Fancy restaurants. Compared to the hustle and bustle of the big city that would be 15,000 kilometres behind them, mother and daughter would lap up paradise.

On such a long flight Sheila would have had many hours to reflect on whether she could have done better. How much had the death of her daughter's father, from a pulmonary embolism during a family holiday in Greece when Heather was just ten years old, affected the child? Sheila's sister, Debbi, tended to agree that it was around that time that Heather began to change from a quiet, lovable child, to a troublesome daughter. At first, Sheila put her daughter's disobedient behaviour down to normal teenage changes, but she became more and more worried about the groups that Heather began hanging around with. She failed to turn up at school, staying out late at night, sullenly refusing to tell her mother who she had been with.

Then there was the missing money. Sheila had no doubt that Heather was stealing from her, sparking shouting matches. It got worse. Physically. Sheila told friends and relatives that Heather had hit her on numerous occasions and while at first the arguments were regarded by others as child–mother spats, Sheila became so frightened that she began calling the police, begging them to come around to the house because her daughter was out of control. Heather's demeanour, one friend eventually revealed, had become explosive. Police recorded 'domestic violence' in their files – yet Sheila refused to press charges against her daughter. But in the nine years that followed James Mack's death, his widow was forced to call the police no less than 80 times to report Heather's violence against her. In one confrontation Sheila's arm was broken and she had to receive hospital treatment.

In one email to a friend to whom she had turned on numerous occasions, Sheila wrote, 'Heather was violent tonight and left. Very scary for me and I am always worried about her.'

In time, Sheila found out that Heather was going out with a 21-year-old African-American called Tommy Schaefer. She had met him a couple of times and believed he was to blame for Heather's increasingly insolent behaviour. She had seen photos on Heather's phone showing the two of them on a beach, she in a yellow bikini, he in a blue T-shirt and grey shorts with his arms wrapped around her from behind. He was, Sheila learned, the reason for Heather staying out until the early hours of the morning and then for her not returning home at all at times. A further insult for Sheila, who had endured so much violence, came when she learned her daughter had 'borrowed' her mother's credit card and had used it to party through the night at the Conrad Hotel in downtown Chicago. She had run up a bill of $1000. Police were called to the hotel and Schaefer was arrested for disorderly conduct.

Heather tried to defend her boyfriend, insisting he was a good person with an impressive academic background. But then Sheila received a further blow. 'I'm pregnant. And Tommy's the father,' Heather revealed defiantly. It was the worst of news. Sheila had hoped she could persuade her daughter to drop the boyfriend who had enjoyed the money that Heather had stolen, and that she would find someone more 'befitting'.

'I want you to get rid of it,' Sheila said, referring to the baby. 'I will not be a grandmother to that man's child.'

Yet another bitter row ensued. And when it was over, after Heather had stormed out of the house again, Sheila decided on one last desperate step that she hoped would lead to the relationship with Schaefer ending and mother and daughter bonding. For her own part, Sheila told friends, she wanted Heather to become the loving child she had once been and for peace to return to her life. She looked to a future in which she would not look upon her daughter as a violent, reckless upstart.

She would take Heather away for a holiday in a place they had never been to before, a peaceful destination that would signal a new start. She'd heard and read about it being akin to paradise. There she would talk to Heather about the baby, try to convince her that the relationship with Schaefer could never last and the child, if it was allowed to come into the world, would end up in a broken home.

As she began working on a solution to all the troubles, Heather and Tommy were also talking. They came up with a plan that would bring an end to Sheila von Wiese-Mack's interference.

The sound of the aircraft engines changed. The jet that had brought Sheila and Heather so far away from all the problems in Chicago was beginning its descent.

Here, Sheila wanted to believe, as the aircraft approached a small island in the Java Sea, was where they could start again.

Bali awaited.

CHAPTER TWO

A COCKTAIL OF LIFE

Street dogs eat rice fit for the gods. Loping towards the small gifts to the Hindu deities laid out on sidewalks in the evening by faithful Hindus, the mongrels and purebreds move in and gobble it all up. But the Balinese are forgiving. They believe that by the time the dogs have eaten their share of the *canang sari,* the gods will have already taken theirs. As darkness falls onto the streets, creeping into narrow alleys where idols of stone glare down, devout Balinese close their doors and are content that their duties in the Island of Gods have been completed.

Stretching just 145 kilometres from east to west, the Indonesian haven – one of some 18,000 islands on the Indonesian archipelago – somehow manages to squeeze in some four million foreign visitors annually, adding to the other four million permanent residents who comprise mostly Hindus, followed by Muslims, Christians and Buddhists who have access to more than 20,000 temples. The number of motor scooters, cars and dogs, who all fight for space alongside people in the towns and cities, can only be guessed at. The chaos that lies in wait: – Massage? Transport? Watches? Hair braiding? You want a girl? A boy? Ganja (cannabis)? – explains why many arrivals prefer to keep the hawkers and the pimps at a distance and laze around their hotel swimming pools for much of their vacation.

For those who decide to leave the resorts behind, Bali offers a cultural feast, with confusion thrown in, confusion that begins the moment they get their bags cleared through customs at the Ngurah Rai International Airport, the third busiest in Indonesia. Rich and poor, scammers, scoundrels, drug smugglers, models and their famed international photographers, all languages of the world on their lips – most pass happily and innocently through immigration and customs. Unless something goes amiss.

On the other side of the immigration and customs checks, a crowd of locals lies in wait: money changers, hotel booking staff, car renters, taxi drivers, drivers waving boards displaying pre-booked guests' names; they all eagerly watch for their prey. The names of resorts and districts, familiar even to those who have never touched down on the island before, are called out by tour guides and drivers: Kuta! Seminyak! Sanur! Ubud!

There's an aroma of incense, spices and petrol fumes in the air – the sweet smell of cannabis is more apparent around the cheap surfie hotels – as the new arrivals follow their driver through the car park to a blue cab. The driver makes small talk: Where are you from? My name is Danny. How long are you staying? Have you been to Bali before? The more experienced traveller knows how to answer and will pretend they know the island well (especially if they have swotted up on their travel guide) for they are then less likely to be taken for a ride, literally and metaphorically. The smart visitor might also pretend that he or she is meeting friends who have arranged all their tours.

Where there was an empty space a couple of years before, another hotel now stands. Bali refuses to stop growing. Top accommodation can run to $1000 a night, while those looking for budget rooms can have a bed and a toilet at the end of a passage for as little as $5.

With its golden beach, stretching on the short side for at least 6 kilometres, Kuta remains the most popular spot in Bali, offering superb surfing, stunning sunsets, beachside bars and restaurants, along with fast-food outlets, convenience stores and street-food kiosks lit at night by oil lamps. You can buy a kite shaped like a galleon or lie under the powerful thumbs of a burly massage lady beneath a sun umbrella. Kuta's nightclubs are packed, its traffic jams choking, but it still remains the most popular area in Bali for 'everyday folk' such as backpackers, surfers and mum-dad-and-kids families.

The 'posh' areas are Nusa Dua, with its string of luxury hotels and, in parts, the hillside village of Ubud, where hotels costing $1000 a night and more offer exclusive accommodation and service for the rich. Personalities who stayed in the village and its surrounds in 2017, strolling through the lush rain forest, included Barack Obama and his family. And the area's secret glades and valleys are perfect locations for photo-shoots. Decades ago, Elle Macpherson was one of the first to be photographed for a magazine shoot in Ubud, dressed in leather and sitting astride a motorbike. I watched her in action at the time and she gave me a cheeky grin.

A COCKTAIL OF LIFE

Despite its sprawling, modern hotel complexes, Bali feels old. The stone gods might have something to do with that impression but in certain parts it's easy to imagine how tiny the place was in bygone centuries, when Hindu priests, noblemen and artisans were fleeing from Muslims on neighbouring Java in the late fifteenth century, resulting in a Balinese kingdom which was to reach the islands lying to the east. But there had been kingdoms long before that, stretching back to the early tenth century and the rule of Buddhist king Sri Kesari Warmadewa, who carved an inscription on a pillar in what is today the Sanur district. His words on the Belanjong pillar, still standing today close to the coral Belanjong Temple, describe how he led a military expedition from Java to establish a Buddhist government in Bali before his army invaded neighbouring islands. As an indication of just how revered the temple remains, handfuls of women arrive there each day in the late afternoon to lay down their small food offerings, just as others before them have done down through the centuries.

Kingdoms and dynasties moved Bali along at a much slower pace than other countries, which wasn't such a bad thing, for many of today's tourists are keen to search out what traces of ancient history remain. Sadly, foreign mariners who fought minor wars with the Balinese plundered many old artefacts. And then in the mid-1800s the Dutch arrived under the flag of the Dutch East Indies, conquering all who tried to resist and swallowing up a number of minor kingdoms. And while a few royal families managed to cling on, the writing was on the wall. Bali lost its independence and the island fell under Dutch colonial control before finally it became part of the Republic of Indonesia. Today Bali stands like a political oasis in the Republic, which controls the world's largest Muslim nation, with the holiday island enjoying its unique position in isolation as a Buddhist domain.

The contrasts between old and new – very old and very new – in Bali are extreme, if you care to look for them. Wealthy, suntanned European women in light summer clothes walk among poor Balinese in their sarongs, each seemingly oblivious to the other. Bent old men supporting themselves on canes are out of place – out of place in their own place – as young European men dash across the beach to throw their surfboards into the sea. And along the waterside strip in Sanur, overlooking the colourful fishing boats that are moored there, small restaurants, coffee machines hissing, serve up every kind of food imaginable, including pizzas.

It's close to 9 pm. At an open-air pizza bar not far from one of the enormous hotels, a blonde English woman, in her late twenties, sits alone with her pizza, a bottle of Bintang beer at her elbow. She was the only customer until I walked in. Her face badly sunburned, she struck up a conversation…the usual: are you staying here? When did you get in? Where are you from?

Angela is travelling on her own. She's from Birmingham and comes to Bali every year. Works in the hotel industry back home and has been able to swing a cheap flight and accommodation. She doesn't do much when she's here. Likes to lie in the sun. Doesn't know anything about the culture or the history or, it seems, anything at all. The conversation doesn't last long. Just long enough for her to drink another Bintang before she says she's going to her favourite place on the beach. It's nice there late at night, she says. She hopes I enjoy my holiday and I say the same to her and then I watch her head across the sand, illuminated by the orange glow of the hotel lights.

I finish my pizza, have another beer and say goodnight to the cook. I look out across the beach. There's Angela, sitting on a plastic chair looking at the dark sea. There's no-one else in sight. Bali is bursting with tourists yet she seems lost. What will tomorrow hold for her? Another meaningless conversation with another stranger somewhere. But then, it's okay to fly to Bali and hang out, doing nothing. Angela was one of many who do it and enjoy it. But as I headed back to the hotel I couldn't help feeling a little sad about how Bali offered so much but for Angela it didn't seem to mean anything at all.

CHAPTER THREE

THE BODY IN A SUITCASE

Nusa Dua, 45 kilometres south of the Balinese capital, Denpasar, prides itself on being the top hotel region in Bali. With its long beaches of white sand, it's a popular destination for those who don't mind paying a high price for their holiday on the Island of Gods.

Claiming to be the best of the best is the five-star St Regis Hotel, where rooms can run to $2000 or more for a night. But guests enjoy all that Bali, and any top hotel in the Western world, can offer. With a driveway entrance that stands beside a rather nondescript road, guests are left breathless as they enter the fabulous lobby with its ball-shaped chandeliers, plush carpets and polished floors. The staff give everyone special attention, as if they are the only guests there.

After an introductory fruit drink, Sheila von Wiese-Mack and her daughter Heather were taken to room 317, which offered ultimate luxury, with a separate lounge area and a wide balcony. A choice of air conditioning or ceiling fans added to guests' comforts. Below, a picture-postcard pool area awaited guests who wanted to do nothing all day but lie around and take an occasional swim. And then there was the beach area, fringed with a line of red sun umbrellas.

Taking in their fabulous surroundings, Sheila might have thought that if she couldn't build a new and loving mother–daughter relationship in this place, then she never would.

After they had unpacked, Heather told her mother that she was going for a walk – the start of a routine which left Sheila perturbed as she would have preferred to be spending more time with her daughter. It is not thought that Tommy Schaefer's name came up at all on the occasions when mother and daughter were able to sit together at the poolside, beside the beach or in the dining room where artistically-presented dishes – lobster, imported prime steaks – were available, along with exotic cocktails. Sunrises and sunsets were breathtaking. The setting was a favourite for Westerners' weddings and for Sheila no surroundings could have been better for her bonding plans.

Sheila might have wondered what could possibly go wrong, although her daughter's frequent disappearances for many hours at a time as the days drifted by continued to be a source of concern.

Then, on 11 August 2014, less than two weeks after the American mother and daughter had arrived, Heather went off for the day and by nightfall had not returned. Sheila watched midnight come and go. Should she raise the alarm? Perhaps Heather had gone to a nightclub or had met a group of people she liked and had dinner with them. The last thing Sheila wanted, on this special trip to patch things up between them, was to give the impression that she was trying to interfere in her daughter's life. She was an adult, after all. But when 3 am came with still no sign of Heather, Sheila decided it was time for action. She hurried through the empty lobby and demanded at the front desk to see the duty manager.

'Have you seen my daughter anywhere?' she asked the manager.

Not in her wildest imagination could she have foreseen the answer. Heather was in the hotel after all. But she was staying in another room. Baffled, Sheila asked for an explanation. A further shock came.

'Madam, you are paying for two rooms. She is there.'

And whose room was it, the stunned mother wanted to know.

'It's a Mr Schaefer.'

According to a staff member, it took a moment or two for the news to sink in. Then Sheila insisted on being put through to Schaefer's room, 616.

'Get down to the lobby this minute,' she ordered her daughter. She knew what had happened – just as it had happened before. Heather had taken one of her credit cards and had paid for Schaefer's room, a plan that had clearly been hatched back in Chicago while, as the days had gone by, Sheila had been working slowly and carefully at bringing her daughter closer to her.

When Heather finally stepped into the lobby her mother pulled no punches.

'So Tommy Schaefer the thief is here?' she cried, close to hysterics.

Heather shrugged, but agreed to return to the room she was sharing with her mother.

'When we get home,' she was heard to tell her daughter, 'I'm going to sue that man for fraud. And who paid for his air ticket to come here? On my credit card as well?'

Heather's silence told her all she wanted to know. The pair returned to room 317, but instead of going to bed, or offering her mother an apology, or at least some kind of explanation, Heather spent the next few hours busily texting Tommy.

It was 8.30 am and other guests were heading to the various breakfast locations in the hotel when the bell of Sheila's room sounded. It was Tommy. He hugged Heather, then turned his eyes towards Sheila. What ensued was a screaming match between the tall man and Sheila, who was dwarfed by his size. Still in her nightdress, she called him a thief and used a derogatory name for a black person.

'You forget, your own husband was black,' he answered back.

'Yes,' Sheila is known to have replied. 'He was black, but unlike you he was rich!'

At first, Tommy laughed – but then he snapped. From under his T-shirt he produced a fruit bowl with a heavy metal handle that he'd brought from his room and swung it hard into Sheila's face. And as she stumbled backwards, arms flailing as she tried to scratch him and push him away, he struck her again and again in the face while she lay on her back. Again and again he smashed the handle into her face, battering so furiously that she became unrecognisable. And then she was still.

While this murderous, bloody scene was being played out Heather slipped away into the bathroom, before Tommy called for her to come out. They hugged. And then he told her, 'Sheila is dead.'

Some days later, a senior police officer opened a thick file of photographs and told me to brace myself as he opened it to a picture of Sheila's face. It was immediately obvious to me why Sheila had died – no-one could have survived such a battering. Yet it wasn't the blows that had killed her. An autopsy had revealed she had choked to death on her own blood, which had flowed down into her lungs.

Heather and Tommy stared down at the blood-soaked body. They needed to do something. They were to claim later that they considered telling the hotel management that there had been a terrible accident but realised such a story would only result in the police being called. So why not, they had discussed, take the body directly to the police themselves? And what would they tell them? There was only one excuse that they could think of: there had been a terrible row and Sheila had attacked Tommy and he had acted in self-defence. Fearing for his life, he had grabbed the fruit bowl and just struck out. Sheila, they could perhaps tell the police, was like a woman possessed, who refused to listen to his pleas to back off. But they couldn't see that excuse being accepted, for Tommy was much stronger than his victim.

They couldn't leave the body in the room. They had to get it out of there and they also needed enough time to flee Bali before the body was discovered. Tommy went back to his room, then returned to Sheila's carrying a silver-coloured. hard-sided suitcase. What followed next was unimaginable.

The two lovers lifted Sheila partially into the opened suitcase, but she was far too big to fit. That wasn't going to stop them. Again, I was later shown a photo of how they had stuffed Sheila into the suitcase. With blood seeping from her ears, nose and mouth and into her blonde hair, they first wrapped her in a sheet before, using brute strength, her bones cracking, they folded her in, bending her forwards so her head was between her legs, which had been folded back towards her ears. It wasn't a perfect fit; they couldn't close the case completely so they retrieved another sheet and used it to tie the lid down as best they could.

It was noon when they took two other bags down to a taxi, but asked a bellboy to push a trolley with the very heavy suitcase down to the lobby. A receptionist who saw red stains on the outside of the suitcase made a remark about it, but Heather said it was 'just make-up stains'. Then, following the bellboy to the taxi, Tommy helped lift the suitcase into the trunk, making an excuse for its weight. They told the driver to wait a moment and they'd be right back after paying their bill. But at the reception desk there was a snag. Heather could not check out because the accommodation was on her mother's card – and Tommy couldn't leave, either, because Sheila had cancelled the card that Heather had used to book him in with. Even worse, Heather couldn't retrieve her passport because it was in a hotel safe box, along with her mother's and only Sheila had permission to open it.

'Are you telling me we can't go?' Heather asked a staff member.

'Not until we speak to madam,' came the reply in reference to Sheila.

There were three ways out of the hotel – through the front entrance, taking a route past the swimming pool and onto the beach or, more dramatically, by scaling a wall. Later, staff were to say that security cameras recorded Heather and Tommy climbing over the wall. At the busy roadside, beyond the oasis that was the St Regis, they waved down another taxi and asked to be taken to the airport. They had return tickets to the US; it was just a matter, they naively believed, of talking their way through immigration without passports. Their wild expectations failed, so they jumped into another taxi and asked to be taken to a cheap hotel. While they didn't have passports – a requirement of all foreign guests checking in – they made up the excuse on registering that they would have them the following day.

Back at the St Regis, the taxi driver was wondering where the guests who had asked him to wait had got to. Idly he looked at the silver suitcase and now it seemed that blood was seeping out through the partially-closed lid. He reported his suspicions to the hotel staff and, confirming it belonged to the American couple who had tried to book out an hour earlier, the management told the taxi driver to take the case immediately to the police. At a local police station, officers reeled when they opened the case and saw the squashed up, bloodied body of a blonde woman.

Soon an island-wide alert was put out for the young couple. The airport and ports were alerted and it wasn't long before word came back that they had already tried in vain to fly out of the country. Police were confident it was just a matter of time before they had the pair in custody. They had no convincing ID, no credit card they could use and a questionable amount of money. The following day officers received the news that the pair were at a budget hotel, some 10 kilometres from the St Regis, having checked in under their own names.

Police raided the room and found the pair still in bed. They had apparently had sex during the night, in between working out what their next move was to be.

As police ordered them to get dressed before leading them out to a waiting car they appeared to show little concern about what had happened.

It seemed they were confident that the story they were going to tell – about Tommy striking Sheila in self-defence, that they had tried to call the US consulate but had heard only an answering machine, that they had panicked at the time but were going to make a full report to the police, that there had never been any intention of killing Sheila – was going to be accepted and they'd soon be on their way back to the United States.

CHAPTER FOUR

MICK JAGGER AND JERRY HALL'S BALINESE WEDDING THAT NEVER WAS

Bali is not only the Island of Gods – it's also the Island of Love. Tourists start romances there, or they travel thousands of miles to confirm their devotion by marriage, to renew their vows, or to participate in an event that they know is ceremonial only, with no legal recognition. They stand together at sunset, once the heat of the day has died, on the beach or beside a luxury hotel pool as friends and relatives snap away with their smartphones, watched by Balinese maidens in traditional costume. It's colourful and memorable, explaining why couples choose Bali to start – or confirm – their futures together.

Everyday folk, as well as millionaires and celebrities share their feelings and make their commitments, most using the services of specialised wedding companies who will have previously advised couples on how to go about a legal wedding, which requires a fair amount of paperwork.

There are high profile couples from around the world who have been married in secret in order to avoid the paparazzi, allowing time to pass before releasing their official photos.

Former Miss Universe Jennifer Hawkins travelled to Bali in 2013 with her fiancé Jake Wall, where they were legally married on a cliff-edge in the peaceful region of Uluwatu. Word of the 'secret' location got out and photographers tried all their tricks to get exclusive shots, but all failed due to extensive security. Taiwanese TV stars Ruby Lin and Wallace were married in Bali in 2016.

Wedding plans were rumoured to have been made by Hollywood A-listers Ashton Kutcher and Mila Kunis, until it was established they had travelled to Bali for a romantic holiday – nothing more. And then there was Kate Moss, who travelled to the island with her family and friends, hoping to be part of a Hindu ceremony with Peter Doherty, until plans had to be cancelled when Doherty was caught up in Britain.

But one ceremony that did go ahead featured two of the biggest show business names in the world – Mick Jagger and Jerry Hall. It was a very hush-hush affair in 1990 but I was fortunate enough to learn about it shortly afterwards and was provided with the finest of details. And I had to regretfully inform the couple, through third parties, that their 'official' wedding was not legal; it was nothing more than a religious ceremony, which would have no binding effect in a British or American court. As it turned out many years later, Mick might have had every reason to thank me for digging around in Bali and unearthing the status of the private Bali ceremony in which he and Jerry had taken part.

While the couple went through the ceremony with sincerity, finding out what it had entailed was more fun than I could have imagined. The rumour – for that was all it was initially – was that the couple had legally married somewhere in the mountain village of Ubud. Establishing the movements of two show business personalities in a Balinese village sounds like a fairly simple affair, but the search to locate someone – anyone – who knew about the ceremony, or had even heard about it, turned out to be monumental task.

The main road through Ubud stretches for miles and then branches out in two directions, leading to hotels and villas that overlook a spectacular valley through which the Ayung River runs. Thankful that I'd set off from my Sanur hotel on a rented motor scooter early that morning – a risky venture with no crash helmet, as they weren't compulsory in those days – I struggled through the thick streams of tooting cars and scooters that filled the narrow road north.

I ate breakfast in the iconic Lotus Cafe, sitting beside a large pond covered with the water plants from which it got its name. That was the first place I began asking if anyone knew about Mick and Jerry being in the village, a question I found myself being interrogated about by excited waiters and waitresses asking me to give them all the information I had. Well, I decided, it wasn't such a bad thing, as they said they'd ask their friends. But I couldn't afford to wait around, and so began a series of frustrating door knocks and visits to other cafes and shops, dropping the name of two of the world's most well-known people. Fortified by countless cups of strong Balinese coffee, I worked my way through the main strip of shops selling batik, T-shirts, kites, sarongs and all types of touristy souvenirs. I was beginning to wonder if the Mick and Jerry wedding was nothing more than a rumour after all.

Then the owner of one of the last shops I tried said something that gave me a slight hope: 'You could try Amir. He knows people.'

It was then a question of finding Amir, who I was told was a woodwork designer, producing top quality Bali-style artefacts. I finally rode into a dusty courtyard, where chickens scratched at the earth and a couple of dogs ran up to sniff at me. A young man hurriedly approached and asked, in broken English, if I spoke Indonesian, before he eventually went off to find out if I would be allowed to go further into what seemed to me to be a sprawling property overlooking a forested hillside.

Amir approached from the main house, a burly man in his forties, dressed in a white shirt and traditional sarong. I asked about the rumour of Mick and Jerry's wedding and, if true, whether he knew where it had occurred.

'Yes of course I know,' he said, almost indignantly. 'It was right here.'

Hiding my surprise, I asked if he would describe it.

'No, no, I cannot do that. Mick is a very old friend. We go back a long time. I cannot betray his trust.'

His refusals and my requests for information went on for some time before he eventually agreed that as it was all over and word would eventually leak out – and perhaps the wrong facts would be spread – he would tell me everything about what was undoubtedly the show-business wedding of the year, and all conducted in the greatest secrecy.

Mick, who was then 47, and Jerry, 34, were dressed in traditional Hindu clothes in preparation for the ceremony, which began with a Hindu priest, Holy Man Ida Banjar, blessing the couple as they stood before him in the large reception area of Amir's house. Then, from a brass bowl, he sprinkled the blood of a sacrificial black chicken onto their foreheads. I wondered how many chickens could have been left in Amir's brood when he described how the meat of five different coloured hens was offered to the gods to keep away evil. A white-feathered chicken was offered to protect the couple from evil from the east, a yellow-feather bird to cover the west, black for the north, red for the south and a mixed-coloured bird for the centre.

Next, Mick and Jerry had to be cleansed. Usually in such elaborate ceremonies couples head down to a river for their cleansing, the wife standing downstream of her husband to wash his clothes, as a symbol of her devotion for the years that were to follow.

'We agreed Jerry and Mick didn't have to do this,' said Amir. 'In any case, the river was too far away. But they still had to be cleansed so they were led to the bath in the house, where they shared a tub of scented water.'

The couple changed into sarongs with yellow brocade tops before declaring their belief in the holy soul, in the supreme being and in reincarnation. They also confirmed their understanding of karma. Their foreheads were daubed with yellow marks, following which Sanskrit prayers were recited by the holy man. Fruit, cake and flowers were offered up, representing the fruitfulness of the couple's union.

The evening was both magical and mystical. The aroma of incense filled the air as the couple sat on a mountain of cushions in the soft glow of candles. The ceremony was far from over. The famous couple were provided with balls of coloured rice with which they touched the sides of their heads and shoulders in the sign of the cross. Jerry was then requested to lay a small raffia mat on the ground after which Mick, now wearing a kris – a sword – was told to approach and pierce the mat with the blade, a symbolic act to signify the union of man and woman.

I'd heard that foreign couples who fly to Bali to be married have to sign a number of legal documents and I asked Amir whether the marriage he had overseen and was symbolic or legal in the eyes of the West.

'That's something you'll have to check out,' he said. 'In the eyes of Hindus, they are now married but I can't say what their status is back in Britain. The person who could tell you that would be at our marriage office.'

That started another search to track down where the marriage office was and who I should speak to. I finally found an official called Widjaya Idabagus who worked at the office of births deaths and marriages – and who happened to be a big fan of the Rolling Stones.

In his office on the outskirts of Denpasar he explained something I already knew – that it wasn't easy for foreigners to go through a legal marriage ceremony on Bali. In most cases at that time couples had to change their religion to the Hindu faith. I told Mr Widjaya that Mick and Jerry had definitely done that, so did it mean the marriage was legal?

'Up to a point…they are on the way,' he said. 'But they have to present to me a document proving they switched faiths and also provide a supporting letter from officials of the temple where the ceremony took place.'

I explained the wedding had not taken place in a temple, but a Hindu priest had officiated.

'They also need to provide me with documents from their consulate or embassy and until I receive all of this they cannot claim to be legally married.'

I also managed to track down the holy man, who couldn't be sure about the legality of the ceremony, but what he did know was that Mick and Jerry had been deeply moved by the experience. 'There was a special aura that came out of them,' he said. 'There was a great spirituality around them that uplifted them.'

As far as I was concerned, based on my conversation with Mr Widjaya, the stars were not man and wife in the eyes of British or US law. After the complex ceremony at Amir's house, the couple had made their way back to an exclusive beachside property at Sanur for their 'honeymoon'. To this day, the villa Batujimbar claims on its website that it was there that Mick and Jerry had married.

The 'union' between the show business icons lasted for nine years, ending in 1999, after Mick fathered a child with Brazilian model Luciana Morad. It was in that same year that it was revealed through Mick's lawyers that he was going to contest Jerry's petition for divorce on the grounds that they were not legally married. She was seeking £30 million from Mick's personal fortune of £150 million. His public relations representatives issued a statement saying the couple 'are not, and have never been, married'. They had been together for 21 years and had four children, but then it was claimed Jerry angrily signed an affidavit alleging that Mick had wrecked the marriage by committing adultery with an unnamed woman. She reportedly referred to him as a 'sexual predator'.

A judge in the British High Court agreed with what I had established years earlier – that the couple were not legally married because they had failed to register the wedding. The judgement was that because it was not valid under Indonesian or English law it should be declared null and void.

I think, by publishing the results of my inquiries over just a few hours in Ubud, I might have saved Mick Jagger a few million pounds. Such unexpected consequences can happen in Bali.

• • •

Big names followed Mick and Jerry to Ubud – Richard Gere, Richard Branson, Julia Roberts – while many others had gone there before, all searching for some kind of fulfilment in a peaceful corner of the world. Charlie Chaplin left his movie walking stick behind and, along with Noël Coward, headed to Ubud in the 1930s to join the small arts community. In fact, Noël wrote a marvellous mini poem for his friend:

> As I said this morning to Charlie
> There is far too much music in Bali.
> And although as a place it's entrancing
> There is although a thought too much dancing.
> It appears that each Balinese native
> From the womb to the tomb is creative,
> And although the results are quite clever,
> There is too much artistic endeavour.

A decade earlier, the Royal Dutch Steam Packet started bringing European tourists to Bali, who soon found their way to what was then the princedom of Ubud. There was no hotel in those days, so tourists had to make do with accepting the hospitality of the locals. The lucky ones managed to find room in a number of bungalows built by Prince Tjokorda Gede Agung Sukawati.

Among the early arrivals from abroad was Walter Spies, a German artist and musician who arrived in the village in 1927 and remained for some 12 years before he became a prisoner of war. Before he was marched off, however, he had inspired scores of young would-be artists whose influence spread to visitors who came in the following decades. The arrivals who didn't paint or write books or poetry were happy enough to live a bohemian lifestyle, talk about love and peace, sit in the yoga position and spend days and nights smoking dope.

CHAPTER FIVE

SHATTERED DREAMS

Did she really know there were drugs in the bag containing her surfing boogie board?

It's a question that has been mulled over since 2004 when then 27-year-old Australian Schapelle Corby was pulled aside by customs officials at Bali airport and asked about the high-quality marijuana packed into a large plastic bag that had been found in the boogie board cover.

'I just saw a plastic bag and thought "This isn't supposed to be here. I didn't put it there,"' Schapelle said in the weeks that followed.

But years later a convicted drug smuggler, Renae Lawrence had insisted, 'She's confessed to me – she said she knew the marijuana was in the body bag,' – a macabre slip of the tongue, for both Schapelle and Renae had at one point faced death and would themselves have ended up in body bags. Many friends of Schapelle – and in fact people who didn't even know her – were to question whether the words of a woman convicted of an even more serious drug offence could be trusted.

Like so many others who have come to grief in Bali, Schapelle's early years back in Australia were filled with disarray. Her mother Rosleigh Rose's marriage to Michael Corby ended when Schapelle was still in nappies, in 1979. Rosleigh, popularly known as Ros, had two other children – Mercedes, born in 1974 and Michael junior in 1976. Rosleigh went on to marry a second time, producing another child, Clinton Rose, in 1984. That marriage collapsed and she went on to marry James Kisina, who had been born in Tonga and with whom she had two more children.

Schapelle remained in her mother's care but they were difficult years and she dropped out of high school in year 11 before starting a beauty therapy course, but failed to complete it. She then worked in the family fish and chip shop and had a second job in a supermarket.

Against this background, the young Schapelle found love with a Japanese man, Kimi Tanaka, who was in Queensland on a working holiday. When his visa expired, he invited Schapelle to visit him in Japan – a promise she kept, and the two finally married in June 1998. It seemed that a brand new future was guaranteed for Schapelle in Omaezaki, Shizuoka. She obtained a job in a Japanese inn, while her husband worked in hospitality. But the marriage crumbled and two years later she was on her way back to Australia. But not directly. She stopped over in Bali, which she had already visited five times, to drop in on her older sister Mercedes, who had married a Balinese man.

Then, on 8 October 2004, Schapelle, age 27, was on her way to Bali once again, her first visit in four years. This time it was with her stepbrother James Kisina, a 16-year-old student, and two friends, Alyth Jeffers (or Ally McComb) a 25-year-old former flatmate of Schapelle's, and Katrina Richards, a 17-year-old kindergarten teacher. The occasion was the upcoming thirtieth birthday of Schapelle's sister Mercedes.

Before taking off from Brisbane airport on a domestic flight that was to take them to Sydney for an international connection, the four of them posed for a photo. Schapelle, with her long black hair running down over her shoulders to her low-cut lime green dress with the image of a large flower on the waist, smiled softly at the camera, oblivious to the horrors of what lay ahead. The photo was taken by Schapelle's mother Ros, who hugged and kissed them all, before the group headed to their flight, QF501.

'We were all so excited,' Ally was to recall several months later. 'We'd worked hard and saved all year. I stopped going out. This was my first trip to Bali.'

As for Katrina, it wasn't just her first trip to Bali – she'd never flown before, and in fact it was the first time she would be away from home for any lengthy period.

James had been to the island before, but it was seven years earlier, when he was nine, to attend the wedding of his half-sister Mercedes to her Balinese boyfriend.

The movements of Schapelle's group, as well as those of all other passengers, were monitored as a routine by CCTV cameras. Images had been picked up of the four checking in their luggage, which included three suitcases and the boogie board in its custom-made fabric carrying case. Schapelle had packed her things, including the boogie board case, at Ros's home in Brisbane, where she and the others had spent the night because they had a 6 am take-off the following morning. Shortly before they were due to leave the house, Ally forgot her flippers and because the suitcases had already been packed and loaded into Ros's car, Schapelle slid the flippers into the boogie-board bag. Schapelle's friends were to insist later that all they saw in the bag as the flippers were being put in was the yellow board.

Sometime around 7.30 am at Sydney airport the group's luggage was moved by baggage handlers to bay 5 at the Qantas domestic terminal, ready for loading onto a trolley to be transferred to the international terminal. Then the bags were taken to pier B at the international airport where the staff checked them to ensure they had been cleared for the scheduled flight. Next, the luggage was passed through a security X-ray before it was due to be delivered by conveyor belt to a bay designated for Australian Airlines flight AO7829. There was, however, a problem with the boogie board – it was too big for the conveyor belt, so it was placed on a trolley and taken to the Australian Airlines bay before being put into a baggage canister containing two of the other bags. Then the canister was closed with a canvas flap, but it wasn't locked. It was kept at the bay, pier C, for more than an hour and a half until, 30 minutes before departure, it was loaded onto the aircraft.

As *The Sydney Morning Herald* was to reveal later, not one of the security camera tapes from the loading areas on that morning of 8 October was checked for images of the boogie board or for any unauthorised approach to the bag. Those images, which were recorded by the cameras, were wiped after four weeks, while those on piers B and C, controlled by the Sydney Airports Corporation, were cleared after 72 hours.

With Schapelle insisting later that she didn't know anything about the marijuana, there could be only one logical explanation for it being in the boogie board bag – unless she had packed it herself, someone, before it was loaded onto the domestic or international flight, had put it there.

The four Australians chatted excitedly as the Australian Airlines jet flew them from Sydney towards their destination. The aircraft was full of other tourists looking forward to a couple of weeks or so in the sun and in a different culture. Bali has always been popular with Australians thanks to its proximity and because it offers such a dramatically different culture.

Seven hours later, in the early part of the afternoon, Schapelle and her companions were walking towards immigration desks at the Ngurah Rai International Airport, still due at that time for its current modernisation. Then they waited at the carousel for their luggage. Ally asked James to help Schapelle with her luggage because she was struggling with her suitcase and the boogie board bag, the latter having been dragged from the carousel by a porter and left on the floor.

Schapelle expressed dismay that the handle on the bag had been broken and the zips were done up in the middle – and she never closed the bag that way. According to *The Courier Mail* newspaper she always zipped the bag up on the side. Ally and Katrina had already gone on ahead through the 'Nothing to Declare' exit, after which they waited for Schapelle and James to come through.

It was a long wait. They were taking forever. Schapelle's friends were not to know then that she and James were having a problem with customs. They had gone to the customs desk in the wake of other tourists and had placed the boogie board bag on the desk for inspection.

Officer Gusti Nyoman Winata was to claim later that he asked Schapelle to open the bag and when he had moved to do so himself she had tried to prevent him. In any case, he said, he asked her whose boogie board bag it was, until it was finally opened. The double-plastic, vacuum-sealed bag of cannabis, about the size of a pillowcase and weighing 4.2 kilograms, was discovered, along with Ally's flippers. That was when Schapelle was to recall thinking, 'This isn't supposed to be here. I didn't put it there.'

What was said between Schapelle and the customs officer was not preserved on CCTV cameras but he was to tell a court later that when he told Schapelle to open the bag she instead opened a front pocket, declaring, 'Nothing in there.' But officer Winata said he wanted her to open the main flap.

'The suspect appeared to panic,' he said. 'When I opened the bag a little, she stopped me and said 'No.' And when he asked why, she replied, 'I have some…'

She looked confused, he alleged.

Looking at the plastic bags inside the bag, he asked what was in them. According to his court testimony she told him it was marijuana. 'I asked her

"How do you know?" She said "I smelled it when you opened the bag."'

The drugs were in a vacuum bag with the brand name Space Bag. It had a nozzle through which air could be extracted and the contents compacted. It had been inserted upside down into another Space Bag. There seemed little doubt that whoever had stuffed the marijuana into the bag had known what they were doing.

In the steamy airport, as all the other passengers made their way out through the exit to be greeted by calls from kiosks where last-minute hotels could be booked, money changed and cars rented, Schapelle and her stepbrother were taken to an interview room. The boogie board cover was laid out on the floor. James was to say later that Schapelle was ordered to wait outside the interview room while he was told to bring the bag in. Whether Schapelle was in the room when the plastic bag was pulled out remained a matter of dispute, but in any case, when she saw it on the floor she recalled recoiling in shock.

Ally was allowed to join the pair some 30 minutes later. 'Oh my God,' she said, when she saw the plastic bag and its contents.

The holiday had turned into a nightmare before it had even begun. Instead of relaxing in her sister Mercedes's home, Schapelle was driven to Kerobokan Prison and locked into a grim, unbearably humid cell. Mercedes had rushed to the airport interview room and, with Ally, had insisted that the plastic bag be fingerprinted.

'Too late,' they were told. 'Too many people have touched it.'

Her sister had tried to comfort her, but Schapelle was inconsolable. The two women spoke about finding the best lawyer to fight charges of importing a commercial amount of prohibited drugs into Bali.

As the days went by the horror that had swept over Schapelle on that first night in the cell would not go away. She realised that if convicted there was a chance she would never leave Bali alive.

Anyone found guilty of possessing and importing the large amount of marijuana that she was going to be charged with was in danger of facing the firing squad.

CHAPTER SIX

GRUESOME EVIDENCE LAID OUT IN THE MIDDAY SUN

The scene was unimaginably surreal. Laid out in the afternoon sun were the trappings of a gory murder. Bloodied sheets, pillows and items of clothing covered the floor of the car park. And there was that silver-coloured suitcase into which Sheila von Wiese-Mack's body had been so brutally crammed. Its 'priority luggage' label, stained with blood, could also be seen. Parked close by was the taxi into which the suitcase had been stowed, two bloodied pillows now on its roof. A stone ornament had been found in the suitcase but it was decided this was possibly something that Sheila had bought as a souvenir. Also on morbid display were what appeared to be two pairs of jeans and a yellow and red cloth item, which appeared to be the same T-shirt that Tommy Schaefer was seen wearing in security-camera footage taken in the hotel lobby.

If I had not known what had preceded this macabre display I might not have given it a second look. But this was the rear of a police station and forensic officers were moving among the items, foraging through them with their gloved hands.

I'd hired an English-speaking driver from the hotel, as I needed him to do some interpreting when I interviewed a police officer I had hoped to ask about progress in the murder. As it turned out, the officer wasn't available. We needed to drive into the parking area in order to turn around and as we did so the driver exclaimed, 'There it is!'

We'd chatted about the case on the way, with him telling me how the entire island had been shocked to learn of the way Sheila had been murdered, and then, as we were about to leave the parking area he pointed out the evidence that the police were going to produce in court. Like washing being draped out in the sun, the sheet and pillows and other items had been laid out in the car park because it allowed plenty of space for the forensic officers to go about their work. It was 17 August 2014, just five days after the murder in the St Regis hotel, and if evidence was needed that the victim had died in a savage attack, here it was.

As expected, I was not allowed to linger. One of the forensic officers approached the car and politely asked me to move on. But I had a chance to ask if this was one of the worst incidents he had worked on.

'See for yourself,' he said. He didn't need to say more and I then had to leave.

Heather had cruelly told her mother before the pair had left Chicago for Bali that she was pregnant with Tommy's child. On the same day that I viewed the 'murder evidence' I learned that doctors in the police hospital to which Heather had been taken had confirmed that she was indeed pregnant and that the foetus appeared to be healthy.

Weeks later, I was sitting in the office of Commander Djoko Hariutomo, who told me that the evidence against the couple was 'overwhelming'. It was he who was to explain how Sheila, 5 feet 5 inches tall, had been folded with brute strength into the metre-long suitcase, with her legs bent up around the sides of her head. And were Heather and her boyfriend co-operating with police, I wanted to know.

'It's a little difficult at present,' the commander conceded. Tommy, it appeared, was obstinate, giving the impression from his police cell in Denpasar that because he was an American he was superior to the police in Bali and it wouldn't be long before he and Heather were released.

Heather, being kept separately at a police headquarters in South Kuta – where I happened to see her being questioned through an open door – appeared to be confused, acting almost child-like. She looked around the room, seemingly uninterested in answering any questions, and played with her fingers. Despite being unable to contact one another, Heather and Tommy appeared to have a telepathic agreement when it came to the food they were provided with.

'They are Americans so we thought we would give them some American food and they would be grateful,' said Commander Hariutomo. 'We gave them KFC but they both said they were insulted to have been offered food that black people would reject on cultural grounds. So now they are eating rice-based local food.' And McDonalds burgers, a particular favourite of Heather's.

In a bizarre explanation for fleeing the hotel, the couple claimed they had run for their lives because Sheila's room had been broken into by an armed gang when they were both inside. 'That wasn't going to work with us,' said the Commander. 'We have a step-by-step replay on CCTV of their movements and they tell a different story to what they are trying to tell us.

'There is little doubt that the attack was premeditated because we have security camera images of Tommy coming down from his room with the fruit bowl under his T-shirt. It was what was used to beat Sheila with. And you know, if the murder had occurred in a cheaper hotel, which would not have such a sophisticated security system, it is doubtful we would have this step-by-step showing of what they did.

'We have the movements of all three parties – the mother, the daughter and Tommy – in all the public areas of the hotel, including the stairways, from the second they checked in on separate days. The evidence, put together from fingerprints, security footage, the behaviour of the suspects, all lead us to believe we have the right people in custody.'

The accused pair received supporting visits from US Embassy officials, as well as American lawyer Michael Elkin. To Mr Elkin, Heather made sensational claims that she had been sexually assaulted 'multiple times' behind bars. The lawyer was to say later that he could not be sure whether she was claiming to have been attacked by prison guards or inmates – if anyone at all.

'It is very disconcerting,' said Mr Elkin after visiting Heather. 'She initially thought it was fellow inmates who had sexually assaulted her, but now she has discovered that not all the guards are wearing official uniforms.'

The arrested pair did little or nothing in their cells. According to Commander Hariutomo they either sat on their beds staring at the walls or glanced at an English language newspaper, looking at the photos and not reading the words.

As the weeks went by, the pair were kept in the separate police stations, having been told that once they were formally charged they would be moved to Kerobokan Prison while they proceed through the laborious Indonesian justice system. It was obvious that Heather, who was nearly two months pregnant, would give birth to the baby while in custody, raising the question as to what would happen to the child. Heather was told that if she was still in prison when the baby was born she would be allowed to keep it in her cell with her until the age of two, when the child would have to be taken into a home on the 'outside' – either in Bali or in the US.

Whispers began to reach Bali that back in the US the couple's names had come up in relation to police investigations there. What would happen if the US authorities wanted the pair back on American soil before they had been dealt with in Bali?

'We aren't taking that into consideration,' Commander Hariutomo told me. 'They are under arrest here. This is our case. They will be dealt with here.'

And he pointed out that aside from security-camera footage that allegedly implicated the two Americans in Sheila's murder, officers had already taken statements from 16 witnesses. 'And that's so far,' he said.

Commander Hariutomo's reference to matters in the US did not detail what they were, but it was clear that he had evidence that made things even worse for the pair he had in custody. For it transpired that there was a third player in the plot to murder Sheila von Wiese-Mack. His name is Robert Ryan Justin Bibbs, a cousin of Tommy Schaefer, and he was involved in a wicked scheme to murder Sheila during her Bali holiday. Text messages between Bibbs and Schaefer were chilling, revealing that they discussed the best way of killing Heather's mother because Schaefer not only hated her, but hoped to become a millionaire from Sheila's death through the inheritance that would come to Heather. Bibbs hoped to cash in on her death, too.

In a text message sent to a friend on 4 February 2014, six months before the Bali holiday, Schaefer wrote that 'she' – a reference to Heather – 'asked me to find someone to kill her mom for 50K.'

Then, two weeks before the holiday, Schaefer texted Bibbs saying: 'She's really tryna [sic] knock her mom off.' A little over an hour later, Schaefer sent another text to Bibbs stating that 'we gotta talk' about 'buckko bucks'.

US Federal officers had no doubts that something bad was in the wind, a fact that Bibbs confessed to later when he told them that he knew Heather wanted to attempt to kill her mother in Bali. In a Federal document quoted by the *Chicago News,* Bibbs said that Heather Mack 'asked me for my advice [on how to kill the victim]…So I told her like "if you would ever do something [to kill the victim], don't get your hands dirty…Don't, don't like grab a gun and shoot your mom.'" The US authorities said that Mack had allegedly told Schaefer in a text message that they should wait until her mother 'passes back out' before trying to kill her.

The chilling messages between Bibbs and Schaefer went further, with Tommy allegedly claiming that an earlier attempt by Heather to kill her mother with an overdose had failed. Bibbs then allegedly suggested that Schaefer should try to drown Sheila in the ocean or 'go sit on her face wit [sic] a pillow then'.

Finally, Schaefer texted Bibbs saying, 'Here I go. Pray for me cuz [cousin].' Bibbs replied, 'Done. It's go time.'

When Bibbs later heard about the murder he sent a text to an unnamed person to say that he felt 'sick to my stomach'. There was possible proof, he said, 'that could lead back to me' and he mentioned the text messages. The other person responded, 'That doesn't make you a murderer.'

If those text messages were shocking enough, Federal authorities were to later release details of scheming messages that passed between Tommy and Heather in the minutes before Sheila was battered to death. Incredibly they found fun in nicknaming each other Bonnie and Clyde, after the notorious 1930s outlaws. And although Schaefer deleted many of the text messages, experts were able to retrieve them.

At 8.20 am on the day of the murder, Heather is alleged to have texted Tommy in his room from the room she was sharing with her mother with the words, 'There's no better time to say hi is there?' The word 'hi' was said by Indonesian police to have been an arranged code for the moment of attack.

'Go with your gut baby…I'll be outside! If u need me I'll hear it,' Tommy wrote.

'Just come here,' she allegedly texted back.

Tommy responded, 'I promise you Heather. All you have to do is get her weak…I'll be standing by the door. Coming now. Relax. Ur Bonnie. Do it.'

Heather wrote back, 'G i think i need you in here too. Okay ill try.'

'Try your best,' he urged her. 'We got nothin to lose right now. Trust me baby. I got you. Can u wack her in the head with a big (expletive) pole.'

'Will she ko,' Heather asked.

'Yes.'

But Heather persisted in asking for Tommy's help in the deadly plan. He responded, 'No, Must knock her out. Must. Listen and shut the (expletive) up already…Ur so stupid.'

According to the authorities, Tommy then sent Heather a photo of the murder weapon – the fruit bowl with its metal surrounds that was in his room. Next Tommy is seen on hotel CCTV footage heading down the fire escape stairs to Heather and Sheila's room. It appears that Heather let him in, allowing him to sneak into a bathroom in the large suite – from where he continued to remain in text contact with Heather.

'Now?' Heather asked, adding, 'Okay slow but don't keep the door open for too long. Too much light comes in. Text when yiure in. Slow g quiet. If i talk at all just come in quick.' [sic]

Eventually Heather wrote, 'Good job. Stay over there. She's facing the other way. Plan?'

Tommy wrote, 'She's so awake.' He might have meant, 'So, she's awake.'

In any case, Heather wrote, 'Sufcte [suffocate] her.'

But Tommy, still in the bathroom, responded with an expletive and the words, 'I gotta hit her.'

Heather had another question. 'Cant we sfcate her together…is that thing [the fruit bowl] hard enough…I'm coming to see it. Im telling her im getting water.'

The final text message, shortly before 9 am according to Federal authorities, came after Tommy had warned Heather that his phone was down to one per cent battery power. In that last message from him he wrote, 'Let me just creep up. And wack her. Once I do it. She was drunk slipped and fell.'

Heather in her final response wrote, 'Okay just knock her out. Itll be so much easier.'

Minutes later Sheila von Wiese-Mack was dead, her face beaten to a pulp, her lungs choked up with her blood.

It was clear from the exchange of messages that while the couple wanted Sheila dead, right up to the last minute they had not prepared a workable plan – nor had they thought about what they were going to do once the murder had been committed. Her beaten face would fool no police officer into thinking she had fallen over while drunk. It is reasonable to assume, too, that the fact Schaefer had carried the murder implement into the room meant he had no intention of overpowering Sheila and smothering her to death with a pillow.

It was those texts that added strength to an already convincing police case against the couple, whose explanation of being attacked by a dangerous gang just didn't hold water. And it was the texts that also formed the basis for the arrest of Schaefer's cousin, 24-year-old Robert Bibbs, who was charged with Federal conspiracy to commit the murder of a US citizen on foreign soil. He, like Heather and Tommy, had believed that Sheila's fortune was as much as $11 million.

Following his arrest, Schaefer sent a text to his cousin telling him, 'For some reason I don' feel bad.' To which Robert Bibbs had allegedly responded that Sheila 'wasn't a good person' and there 'wasn't any positive energy released from her body'. Dismissing the seriousness of the event in Bali, Bibbs had sent Schaefer another text some two minutes later in which he had joked about being overlooked for the US men's national basketball team.

The *Chicago News* noted that, 'That kind of callous disregard for human life is littered throughout a 29-page criminal complaint…after federal authorities arrested Bibbs in Chicago and identified him as a previously unknown player in von Wiese-Mack's sensational murder.'

Robert Bibbs was far from happy at being linked to Sheila's slaughter. Faced with life in prison if convicted, he glared at bystanders as, wearing a faded 'Coke' T-shirt, he appeared in court for the first time. When it was time to tell his story about what happened in Bali and his connections with it, he told the Chicago court that Heather had offered him $50,000 to kill her mother. Now wearing blue corduroy pants and a white button-down shirt, he turned away from such an offer and said that he had instead advised Heather and Tommy how to fatally drug or suffocate Sheila.

'Heather kept expressing how she hated her mom and how they always fought,' said Bibbs, pleading guilty to his advisory role in the killing. 'I really didn't expect (my cousin) to do anything like this…it's very unflattering.'

Bibbs was facing the rest of his life in prison, but under an agreement with the prosecution he settled with 'not more than 20 years' in exchange for pleading guilty to conspiring to commit the murder. In addition to his murderous advice, it transpired, he warned Heather and Schaefer to be careful about surveillance cameras – a caution that the couple had clearly forgotten about.

Back in Bali, Heather and Tommy went through the court process, being dealt with separately, although they arrived together at the court complex in an armoured prison van along with other inmates. Wearing orange prisoner vests, they hugged one another as they stepped out before being led to separate cells, directly opposite one another, in the courtyard.

It was easy enough for me to ask Heather questions – What outcome was she hoping for? How was the baby she was carrying? Did she have any regrets? – but my words fell on deaf ears. She had eyes only for Tommy in the cell opposite, blowing him kisses, which he did to her in return. Sometimes she would sit with other female prisoners on a bench at the rear of the holding cell exchanging whispers with them as a throng of photographers took their shots. She was an easy target, after all.

It was also an opportunity for an Australian woman who had befriended her to pass food to her and just show that she was there to support her. The young woman declined to say how she had entered into Heather's life, but it was clear from the way the American always greeted her that a strong bond had been formed.

Heather had her dramas as the weeks and months passed and remands came and went for her and her boyfriend. On at least two occasions she had to be rushed to Sanglah Hospital amid fears there was a problem with the baby she was carrying, but the emergencies were soon put to rest and she was returned to her cell, which she was sharing with up to ten other women, in Kerobokan prison. Word leaked out, however, that some of the women in the cell were not happy to learn that she intended to keep the child with her in the prison for the two years that mothers were allowed before their babies had to be passed out to carers. They told her they were concerned a newborn baby would keep them awake, but their anger eventually died down.

Throughout her trial, in which she had pleaded not guilty to premeditated murder, the strain showed on Heather's face, as she followed proceedings through an interpreter. There was added drama when her lawyer withdrew from the case citing a 'substantial breakdown in communication'. At one point, Heather made a phone call to a clerk in the US office of Cook County judge Neil Cohen, saying she needed help with an attorney, following which the judge informed her she could use some of the money her murdered mother had left in a trust fund for her.

Back again in a holding cell, she answered a few questions and claimed that she missed her mother every day and loved her 'with all my heart'.

In March 2015 Heather was taken to hospital and gave birth to a daughter she named Stella, after Tommy's great-grandmother. 'I know I'm going to be found not guilty of this,' she said later, cradling her baby as she sat in the holding cell. 'It's going to be okay for us.' And she dismissed suggestions that she could face the firing squad if convicted of premeditated murder. 'It's not going to come to that,' she said.

Finally, it was her turn to tell her story to the judges, repeating Schaefer's own defence that he had hit Sheila with the fruit bowl in self-defence while she, Heather, had hid in the bathroom – a story that was in conflict with the text messages that had passed between the two. The blow was not so hard, she said, and her mother was fighting back. 'I asked Tommy to stop and then I ran into the bathroom. When I came back out Tommy was on the bed trying to give my mother artificial respiration. He said she wasn't breathing. I tried to revive her but it didn't work.'

'Did you wish your mother dead?' one of the three judges asked.

'No,' she replied.

On Tuesday, 21 April 2015, Heather Mack, 19, and Tommy Schaefer, 21, escaped the death sentence when three judges sentenced her to 10 years imprisonment and Schaefer to 18 years. Both wept as the sentence – far lighter than many had expected – was handed down.

In the US, Sheila's sister, Debbi Curran, of St Louis, told the *Chicago Tribune* that the punishment did not fit the crime. She told how Sheila had filed dozens of complaints against her daughter for battery, theft and truancy in addition to missing person reports.

'My sister when she was alive was bruised, bitten and even had her arm broken by Heather and yet she loved her unconditionally and never gave up hope that Heather would be better.'

After the verdict Heather and Tommy were led back to their cells, where Heather would continue to nurse her one-month-old baby…but the drama that had followed the pair in Bali was far from over.

CHAPTER SEVEN

BALI'S OTHER 'HOTEL' – KEROBOKAN PRISON

'I have never stayed in the Seminyak/Kerobokan area, but we are this time. I have been told that the prison wall is only a couple of hundred meters from the villa we are in. Has anyone stayed near the prison? Did you even notice it?'

'Hi, we are staying in Kerobokan in a friend's village. We have two children. I am a little concerned with Kerobokan. I basically just wanted to know if it is safe…'

'Hi, we are looking at a villa on the same street and have been told by the owner that the jail is at the opposite end of the street. I just don't like the "vibe" of having a prison too close by, but if we never have to pass it, it might be okay?'

'Noise would be my main worry. After huge prisoner riots last year where prisoners locked out all the guards, threw Molotov cocktails over the walls and torched the jail, a new multi-million dollar building at the front is currently being built…It is easy to get taxis to anywhere and some of the best restaurants are only a minute or two drive away.'

Westerners who have lived in Bali for any length of time have become accustomed to the questions asked about the proximity of Kerobokan prison to holiday homes and, in fact, how near it is to the popular tourist areas of Bali, particularly Seminyak. And in more recent years, as the tourist regions have fanned out from Kuta, Legian and Seminyak, they have begun to embrace the district of Kerobokan, where the prison with the most notorious reputation in Indonesia stands, a sombre monument to crime just a ten-minute taxi ride from the luxury hotels of Seminyak. And in a bizarre way, while many vacationers want to stay well clear of the steel gates and blue-grey, mould-stained walls of Kerobokan with their razor-wire tops, the prison has become a tourist attraction. Overseas visitors turn up daily to take selfies and have even cheekily asked guards and police to pose with them. It's ghoulish in every respect, for beyond the walls are men and women who will spend the rest of their lives there or who have a death sentence hanging over them, terrified that the time will come when they will be led out of their cells and transported to the prison island of Nusakambangan to face a firing squad. The 'look at me outside Kerobokan prison' photo opportunity actually has a bad look.

The jail rises up in the centre of a busy residential area from which it gets its name, and is close enough to the main holiday strip for it to earn the description of a 'hell hole that rubs shoulders with paradise'. If there were a tower a little higher than those used by guards it would be possible to see the ocean.

It's a curious place, for it houses the worst of the worst, yet first-time visitors are often surprised at the 'village' atmosphere, particularly in the women's section. Female prisoners sit outside their cells, chatting to their 'neighbours' while doing their washing using plastic buckets and hose pipes. Prostitutes, drug pushers, murderers…they have found a social level, making all equal.

The men's side is a harsh contrast, an area where frightening home-made knives have been found, drugs are passed around – having been brought in by corrupt guards – and fierce fights break out between rival gangs. Not that such events don't occur on the women's side. Indonesian and international prisoners linger in Kerobokan, waiting for their trials to come up, or while away the hours painting, writing letters, working in the kitchen, sticking needles into their arms, sucking on meth pipes or shaping furniture in the workshop before sending their craft – sometimes containing hidden drugs of all kinds – out to be sold by contacts who would simply destroy it to get at the narcotics. The drugs come in, they get shared around, and out they go to other users.

Kerobokan – 'Hotel K' – known in Indonesian as Lapas Denpasar, opened in 1979 and was intended to hold some 300 prisoners. Today the number is closer to 1200, explaining why up to 10 inmates are forced to share one cell. At least there is a prison there now, along with two others in Bali, reducing the risk involved in moving criminals to jails in Java. The country's 441 prisons were categorised by the number of inmates each could hold. The nine largest housed prisoners who were sentenced to life imprisonment or death.

Located in Java were several specialised jails for women, along with two for youths. But sometimes it wasn't possible to move this category of prisoners to these particular jails and they had to be locked up in the main prisons. Today the prisons of old still stand as Indonesia's population continues to grow to more than 260 million, so while Bali holds a fraction of the country's prisoners, its crime rate is on a par with the rest of Indonesia.

The offences for which prisoners in Kerobokan are detained belie the unblemished image that the island portrays in the tourist brochures – and a number of those crimes involve tourists. Theft is a major problem, be it from handbags or muggings, although face-to-face confrontations with Westerners are rare. Prostitution is growing to meet the increasing numbers of male tourists, but among the visitors come the paedophiles, despised by all.

Children from poor Asian families are easy targets and youngsters in Bali are no exception. Until a few years ago, sleazy hotel proprietors would arrange for a young boy or girl to come to a paedophile's room, often with the parents' blessing because they needed the money. In more recent times, mainly due to the urging of overseas law enforcement agencies, the hotel rendezvous between Western paedophile and Balinese child has been interrupted, but the molesters who end up in Kerobokan are evidence that they are still out there.

Inmates stare at you as, after all the paperwork for a visitation has been stamped, you walk from a waiting area into the jail itself. The prisoners wonder who you are – embassy, friend, lawyer, journalist? – and who you've come to see. Other inmates will throw a glance before turning away, not wishing for eye contact. There's an unmistakable air of mistrust among the inmates. It's not the most comfortable place for a foreigner to meet a detainee with a floor of concrete and a tin roof, but family and prisoners are just happy to see one another. The men will tell you how tough it is; or at least most will, apart from a boastful few who insist they can handle anything the Balinese jail system can throw at them.

Just look at the case of Julian Ponder, a convicted British drug dealer, who claimed he could get anything he wanted, including the affections of a female diplomat tasked with liaising with him. The Western prisoners will tell you of the imbalance of sentences for various crimes: deal with heroin or cocaine and you can get the death sentence, or at best, life; murder someone and you might get only a few years. The severity for drug offences is clearly aimed at deterring others who try to traffic in the hope that fewer crazed people will be walking the streets. Why a murderer should be let out after a relatively short time still angers and confuses those who are serving many years for narcotics.

Despite what the men will describe as a hell on earth, with an ongoing threat of a beating, a stabbing, contracting a dreadful disease and night upon night with little sleep in a crowded, mosquito-ridden cell, there's one jail visitor who insists that, certainly on the women's side, Kerobokan is far from squalid. Lizzie Love, a long-time resident of Bali, volunteers to help and guide female prisoners and she's said time and again that things could be far worse. The jail, she says, has been given an unfairly bad image. The women can turn their cells into a home away from home, or at least a room away from home, and for those who can afford to pay the officials they can use computers and even log onto Facebook. The women make creative jewellery, paint their fingernails, do work in the jail's office and listen to music on their iPods.

On both sides of the 'his and hers' fence religious services are on offer and there have been times when agnostic Western prisoners have found solace in one of the Indonesian faiths – either Hindu, Islam or Buddhism. Sometimes, though, prayers aren't enough and prisoners go through day after day wishing it had brought good news. They all know that life means life. There's no parole. If all appeals fail, they only walk out if there's a royal pardon.

But while Lizzie Love insists that Kerobokan isn't as bad as has been made out, New Zealand-born Paul Conibeer tells of ten months of horror in what he says is one of the only jails in the world where the prisoners are in control. At the age of 43 Conibeer, by then working as a car salesman in Blacktown, New South Wales, flew to Bali in August 2012 to have a big party, in which he would sink into the Bali bar scene – just as he had no less than 30 times before. But things went wrong. He was robbed outside a nightclub, and if that wasn't bad enough, he became involved in a row over an unpaid hotel bill. Before he could even try to sort it all out he ended up in Kerobokan. His new 'mates' were killers, paedophiles and rapists – 51 of them in a cell meant to hold no more than 33.

'Bali is not what you see in the tourist brochures,' he was to relate on his release. 'It remains dangerous and corrupt – a trap for the young, the naive and those, like me, who wanted to have a good time at the expense of common sense.'

Among the nightmare scenes that continued to haunt him on his release was the time he nursed a dying man and another time panicking as he watched his rotting toenails drop off. As for drugs, they were all through the prison with prisoners tripping out on LSD or magic mushrooms and smoking weed 'until they were stoned blind'.

They do have to eat, though. Officially, prisoners receive basic rice-based meals, but if they can afford to send out for food – and Westerners mostly do – there's no problem arranging for a takeaway at one of the small restaurants across the road from the prison.

The daily, weekly, monthly, yearly routine in an environmental sauna can cause tensions. A wrong word, a misunderstanding, a thrown punch and in no time there's war.

A riot broke out in December 2015 when warring gangs set on one another with knives, spears and machetes, resulting in four people dying. More than 100 prisoners were moved to other jails on the island, including a new prison for narcotics offenders. Incredibly, a number of garbage bins were also found to contain methamphetamine, a computer and a home-made bulletproof vest. Riot squad police who reached the prison established that the troublemakers were members of two opposing criminal groups – Laskar Bali and the Baladika gang – but it seemed the spark for all the trouble was the difficulty Laskar Bali members were having getting into the prison to see members of their families.

The following year the riot squad were back again after members of the Laskar Bali gang were allowed into the prison. Hatred between the two gangs who had fought before had not died down and when officials allowed 11 members of Laskar Bali to enter on a visit, trouble erupted. This time, no-one was seriously injured. Made Badra, of the Bali Corrections Office told Fairfax Media, 'We told the prosecutors not to put them in Kerobokan jail because last December there was already an agreement that Laskar Bali people should not be put in Kerobokan. But prosecutors insisted.'

This is what happens in Bali. Some people listen; some don't.

CHAPTER EIGHT

THE BREAKOUT

Of one thing he was certain – they weren't going to deport him to Australia. No way. Back on Australian soil it would be court and another jail. And despite his current surroundings in Bali – a crowded cell with 20 other prisoners – he'd heard that an Aussie jail would be much tougher because the strict rules would take away all the fun.

Shaun Davidson had heard about the tunnel in Kerobokan prison. He knew that it was being used to smuggle in drugs right under the noses of the woefully inadequate contingent of eight guards. But he hadn't heard of anyone using it to escape because it was full of sewage. In fact, how anyone actually got through with drugs was a mystery to him. But as time drifted by towards the date when he would be released, he thought more and more about the tunnel. If he could use it to get out of Kerobokan, then he might be able to disappear and avoid ending up in another jail in Australia.

Davidson, 33, had been arrested and charged in Perth in January 2015, accused of a number of offences including possessing narcotics with intent to sell. When he failed to turn up in Perth Magistrate's Court a warrant was issued for his arrest. He couldn't be found – because he had flown to Bali on the very same day. And he was going to make the most of his freedom on his one-month tourist visa. He sparred in boxing clubs where the locals admired his skills but there were many more hours spent just partying. From punching bags in the gym, he hit the clubs of Kuta and Legian at night, aware that one day it would surely all come to an end.

Men on the run who still want to have fun need a change of identity and the opportunity to become someone else presented itself when he 'found' a tourist's passport in a hotel. It had, in fact, been reported missing back in 2013. Perhaps unaware of the fact that its loss had been reported, he used the passport to sign into the three-star Rabasta Beach Resort in the Tuban area, explaining that the photograph had been taken when he looked more chubby. But with the passport having already been reported missing by its real owner and the fact that the visa in it was well past its expiry date, Davidson's Bali holiday was as good as over. Authorities were alerted to a 'possible visa overstay' and police came to collect him.

At Denpasar District Court in August 2015 Davidson was jailed for 12 months and fined 100 million rupiah ($9500) for not only overstaying his own visa but for using a false identity. The head judge, Made Pasek, said he found the Australian 'convincingly guilty', although he noted that Davidson had been polite during his trial and had readily admitted his guilt. The judge added, however, that the 'overstayer's' use of false documents was harmful to Indonesia. Davidson said afterwards that jail was not what he had been hoping for 'of course', but 'I think it is a fair judgement.'

Despite the crowded surroundings, he soon settled into prison life and even started to boxing train up to 20 inmates. His relationship with the locals led to him making a number of important contacts and it was through them that he learned of the tunnel. Police were later to suspect that Davidson began secret negotiations with an 'escape syndicate' who would not only help him from the jail but out of the country. Even if that was true, senior officers were later to agree, he would need money – lots of it – to pay for his freedom, and where would he get that?

Meanwhile, Davidson was plotting with three other prisoners in between giving boxing lessons. 'That's pretty good,' he said of his training. 'I guess it gives the locals something to do. It gives them something to look forward to. It's pretty hard for some of the locals – if you don't have money to get food, you don't eat.'

In mid-June 2017 came the dramatic news that Davidson and the three others he had been plotting with – Bulgarian ATM skimmer Dimitar Nikolve Ilieve serving 7 years; Indian Sayed Mohammed Said, a drug smuggler serving 14 years; and Malaysian drugs offender Tee Kok King serving 7 1/2 years – had escaped from Kerobokan. They just weren't anywhere to be found the following morning, having been locked in their shared cell the night before. It wasn't long before an inspection around the outside prison walls found a narrow, water-filled hole. It was hardly wide enough to take a man, yet it became apparent this was the way out. An investigation on the inside of prison found a sewerage tank, from which a pipe ran, joining up with the hole which appeared to have been dug from the outside. The escapers had undoubtedly received help from the other side of the prison walls.

The hole, however, was full of filthy, grey sewage water and there were concerns that the missing men might all have remained trapped – and drowned – in there. A prisoner agreed to a police request to squirm through the hole, holding his breath, to check it out. He emerged, covered in sewage, beyond the wall to confirm there was 'no-one else in there'.

With Bali being a small island police believed it would not be long before the prisoners were caught. Ports were put on watch, as was the airport. It was also suggested that the four men would simply lie low for as long as it took before eventually making their escape. What police did not realise was that two of the group – the Bulgarian and the Indian – had gone virtually straight to the airport after clambering out of the tunnel, changing their clothes and flying out of the island. It was suspected that Davidson had done the same, although the exact whereabouts of all escapers remained a mystery.

Then came a breakthrough – the Bulgarian and the Indian had been arrested on 22 June, three days after they had fled, in neighbouring East Timor, formerly a part of Indonesia. They had been trying to find a boat to sail them to yet another country. Chief Superintendent Henrique da Costa of East Timor Police told *The Sydney Morning Herald* that the two had earlier been staying at the $4\frac{1}{2}$ star hotel Novo Turismo Resort and Spa in Dili. They had arrived in East Timor by boat two days earlier from the Indonesian island of Alor in East Nusa Tenggara, it was believed.

In order to establish exactly how the four had escaped, including getting out of their cell, prison authorities and police arranged for a re-enactment, a popular way throughout South-East Asia of establishing in detail how a crime had been carried out. Two of the 'stars' of the re-enactment would be the re-arrested men, Dimitar Ilieve and Sayed Said, following their return in handcuffs to Bali on 25 June from their short-lived holiday. They looked far from happy as they were led back to the prison in the company of masked riot squad police with their automatic weapons.

Before any re-enactment could begin, however, the men were grilled on who had helped them on the outside, for indeed they had received an enormous amount of assistance, with an empty building nearby to change into clean clothes awaiting them, transport to the airport, false passports, and money to pay their way to freedom.

'We are going to get to the bottom of this,' the island's chief of police, Inspector Petrus Golos resolved. 'If we don't cut off the head of the beast the syndicate will continue working to free other prisoners.'

As a start, police managed to track down a former prisoner who had bought the air tickets for the escapers and who had helped them check in at the airport. Not only was he charged with assisting the break-out, but he was also told he would be required to take part in the re-enactment.

It took the best part of three weeks for the replay of the escape to be arranged but finally the two recaptured prisoners, the former prisoner, jail officials and police officers crowded into the cell. Officials had already established that the tunnel began from within a sewerage tank, but they still wanted to see the recaptured men go through the routine. Such a brazen escape had been planned for weeks, timed to take place at night.

At 10 pm on 18 June, the four men had scrambled through a hole in the ceiling of their cell and under cover of darkness had made their way to the rear of the prison medical centre, where the tunnel began. They had chosen this particular night because it was pouring with rain and it was unlikely there would be any guards wandering around. But the rain had brought a problem for the escapers – the water in the tank had risen and had gushed into the tunnel. No-one was going to crawl through that narrow tunnel in the dark with the very real danger of drowning, so they used plastic buckets, on hand for this very reason, to bail water from the tank and the hole. It took them more than four hours before Davidson became the first man to start crawling through. This was uncharted territory. The escapers had only the word of others that it was possible to wriggle through. If anything went wrong or if they'd been given wrong information, such as the tunnel being blocked at the exit, they would certainly drown.

One by one, they squirmed up through the exit, the width of a man's shoulders, pushing out with them a collection of rubbish – plastic bags, bottles, cans – that had found their way into the hole over time. An overweight prisoner would not have made it through that small hole. Their outside help – it is not known whether this was more than one person – led the group to an empty building across the street, where they pulled their dry clothes from plastic bags before catching a cab to the airport.

The replay of the escape, with the Bulgarian and the Indian playing themselves, with their names attached to signs on their orange prison uniforms, had fascinated all the watching officials. This time, while they had to show how they escaped through the cell ceiling, the recaptured men did not have to go through the tunnel but watched in amusement as the prisoner volunteer and later a police officer crawled through, emerging covered in grey slime.

With two of the prisoners back behind bars the question arose as to the whereabouts of Davidson and the Malaysian, Tee Kok King. At first it was thought that they had also made their way to East Timor but there was no sign of them there. Then a cheeky Facebook message in the name of Matthew Rageone Ridler, Davidson's alter-ego, came to light. Just like a former Australian escapee years before who taunted police with postcards while on the run, 'Ridler' claimed to have been in Amsterdam, Germany and Dubai. However, there were no photos of him in any of the posts. In an update, he denied that he had been taunting police or that he was a public threat — as stated by Interpol — but he did thank all international officials for taking an interest in him.

'I'm not, as the media says, taunting police and I'm definitely not a public threat, as Interpol would have u believe,' he wrote. I'm just having some fun and a laugh. I'm living my life just trying to make the best out of a bad situation. It's always better to laugh than anything else. Also, I'd like to thank the police and Interpol for taking an interest in me and putting in your time and hard work thanks guys well done.'

On 19 July 2017, 'Ridler' decided to turn to poetry, writing, 'I've been a free man now for 30 full days, I've left fans amazed, police and governments dazed, who wouldv [sic] thought I'd be on top with my cheeky smartass ways.'

His life on the run resulted in a build-up of fans. One even tried to raise $50,000 to keep him running before the funding site was shut down. Speculation was rife about where the runaway really was, but one of the most popular guesses was that he had made his way to Thailand's sleazy resort town of Pattaya, where a number of international fugitives and bad boys had set up home.

Bali jail officials remained adamant that Davidson and Tee Kok King would be back behind bars before long. The fact two of the escapers had been quickly caught gave international agencies confidence that the Australian and the Malaysian would soon be recaptured.

'We are tracing their footprints,' declared Mr Ruddi Setiawan, deputy director of special crime. 'The two men will be caught.'

Ironically, officials said that if and when the runaways were recaptured they would not be charged with escaping. But they would face charges for damaging prison property when they widened the getaway hole.

On 22 August 2017, police announced that they were closing in on Davidson because they had established that, despite his alter ego claiming he was in various parts of the world, he was actually still in Indonesia.

'He is the focus of a search between Indonesia and Timor-Leste,' said Bali provincial police chief Petrus Golos. 'We think he has been trying to get into that country, following the others who escaped there before their recapture.'

Mr Golos repeated the words of other officers when he said he was confident Davidson would be in handcuffs very soon.

But the farcical situation moved up to a new level the very next day, 23 August, when News Limited in Sydney received a message, purportedly from the fugitive, stating that he was nowhere near the border of Indonesia and East Timor. He was clearly keeping watch on the news – and keeping himself in it.

He claimed he had left Indonesia because he was afraid he would be shot by police.

'Them still thinking I'm in Indonesia is the best thing for me so they can keep looking and thinking I'm there, I'll only be shot if I get caught inside Indonesia by Indonesian police and resist arrest none of those things will happen, I'm not Indonesia so their police can't and when and if ever Interpol come knocking I'm not gonna resist I've never resisted arrest,' said a verbatim version of the message.

If Davidson was behind the dispatch – and not someone writing on his behalf – he made it known that he did not have faith in the system in Australia where charges awaited him. He did not have faith in receiving a not guilty verdict.

'The courts will believe one police officer over evidence from someone with a criminal history, even if the evidence proves not guilty or if there's no evidence to prove guilt.'

He told the news group that he wanted to live the rest of his life happily – he was living a normal life 'in a new place and am happy doing so'.

He joked that it was very entertaining being able to post locations where he was, leaving everyone, including police, to believe the claims were not real.

His new hideaway, he claimed, was Barbados, and in his message, he posted a map of the First Fitness Gym in Oistins, Barbados, before noting it was, 'Dinner time I'm starving.' He also posted a map of Cafe Luna Barbados.

It is doubtful that anyone would be prepared to bet that he would be found sitting there.

CHAPTER NINE

THE 'PRECIOUS ONE' AND THE ENGLISH MODEL

It wasn't quite an Ursula Andress in *Dr No* moment, but the woman who walked out of the Bali sea had a certain 'something'.

'You must be Susan,' I said as she came towards me in her bikini. 'And if you're not, you're a very good body double.'

She laughed and said, 'Yes, I'm Susan.'

Susan Sarandon continued walking into the grounds of the Oberoi Hotel, hesitating for the briefest of moments as if expecting me to ask her for her autograph. But I wasn't going to impose. She was in Bali for a vacation and, like so many other celebrities who have quietly come and gone, she wasn't going to wave any flags.

Afterwards, once they're back on home soil, yes, by all means let the world know what fun they've had and even post a few selfies. And few holiday snaps could be more sensational than that of American singer and composer John Legend and his wife Chrissy Teigen. Their photo, taken in a secluded villa near Ubud, gives an immediate impression that these are the true rulers of Bali. Dressed in stunning royal robes of purple and gold and with John clutching a sceptre while Chrissy holds a fan, they were reminiscent of the rulers of old. With her father being of Norwegian descent and her mother being Thai, Chrissy's part-Oriental looks added to the regal illusion.

'We had the most beautiful, wonderful time in Bali,' John wrote on Instagram. Fans of the winner of ten Grammy awards, a Golden Globe award, a Tony, and yet another gong from the Songwriters Hall of Fame would no doubt agree that the couple could have passed as royalty anywhere in the Island of Gods.

A British model had dressed in such finery years earlier for her marriage to a Balinese prince, a fantastic, colourful wedding the exclusive story details of which one of the leading UK newspapers paid a reported four-figure sum for. The tale of beautiful Marianne Roy's wedding was picked up by magazines and newspapers around the world, for it was a rare, if not unique, event indeed for a Westerner to marry into Balinese royalty. The British paper announced that through the marriage, during the ceremony for which she had worn a crown of gold, Marianne had become one of the highest-ranking members of the Bali royal hierarchy and from the moment the vows had been taken she was elevated from being plain Miss Roy to be known as Princess Maitre Vairokani Dewi of Pandji.

But there was much more than a title. She would, *The Daily Telegraph* announced, have the choice of eight magnificent palaces to live in, where bowing servants would attend her every whim, while in the streets and temples her subjects would throw themselves at her feet. Understandable for a woman who had married a demi-god known as The Precious One, Prince Sri Acarya Vajra Kumara Pandki Pandita, a twelfth-generation descendant of the enlightened King Pandji Sakti of Singharaja. His friends, and only his very closest friends, were allowed to refer to him with a shortened version – Ratu.

In a modest concession, Ratu made it known that he would not take up his constitutional role, but would instead act as a spiritual adviser to his people. Having learned a fair amount about Westerners getting married in Bali following the revelations about Mick Jagger's wedding to Jerry Hall, I began to smell a Ratu about Marianne's glorious wedding, which had left the world gasping. It didn't take long for me to find out that the old King of Bali, who was said to have given his blessing to the pair, could not have done so – unless his ghost had returned – because he had died many years earlier. There was much more embarrassment to follow…

Marianne's story had begun in 1996, during an educational trip to the US, when, in a club in Santa Fe, New Mexico, she met Ratu, a 42-year-old divorcee who was propping up the bar with a group of friends. According to Marianne, it was love at first sight; she was smitten by his exotic good looks.

'We all ended up at a friend's house and we just got talking,' she told another UK newspaper in a reportedly paid interview. 'We talked for most of the night about Buddha and Ratu told me that, as the lotus flower grows from the mud but remains unstained, so does compassion, love and kindness grow from understanding suffering rather than cursing it.'

More of her background was to follow in the story that unfolded in the newspaper. At 16, she said, she had been raped but because she was 'too young and too embarrassed to do anything about it', the attacker escaped prosecution. All her English boyfriends, she told the UK press, 'just used and abused me – sex always seemed dirty to me'.

There followed a six-year struggle against anorexia and bulimia, during which her 175 centimetre frame shrivelled to just 47 kilograms. Despite such handicaps, she sailed through her A-levels and was offered the chance of obtaining a fine arts degree in London. And it was during an exchange trip to study Native American art that she met up with the Balinese man who was to make all her dreams come true. He told her of all the wonders that awaited her if she would come back to Bali with him and be his wife. Marianne could hardly believe her good fortune and promptly abandoned her studies and moved first to Melbourne, where Ratu was teaching Buddhism. Marianne enlisted with a local modelling agency. Talk of marriage continued, with Ratu explaining that their wedding would be blessed by his uncle, the King. And the ceremony would take place in the Orchid Palace. Recalling the event, Marianne said that 'everyone who was anyone was present. The King and Queen were there, the High Priest, Ratu's father and all his friends. There was incense and flowers and I was drenched in holy water. The ceremony went on for six hours but I'll remember it for the rest of my life.'

If any wedding had the same feeling as Mick Jagger's 'ceremonial only' marriage to Jerry, it was Marianne's betrothal to her Prince. The *Daily Telegraph*, however, believed every word of the genuineness of the wedding, overflowing with a description that said Marianne 'looked a template of nuptial loveliness; bare-shouldered and carrying white roses. He with his slipper black, Disraeli-like curls and Victorian wing collar, seemed to have strayed from the sub-plot of a Dickensian novel.' There was more. For someone so recently transplanted from student to royal personage, 'Princess Marianne maintains a remarkably cool demeanour. This may, of course, be because she was a princess all along. The old king of Bali clearly thought so; after their blessing, their union, he turned to Marianne and said, "Welcome home."'

The wedding was rich in colour and, it transpired, hard cash, for in Australia a magazine paid the couple an estimated $30,000 for an interview and photographs. This time came Marianne's claim, speaking now as Princess Maitre Vairokani Dewi of Pandji, that she was a direct descendant of Rob Roy, despite that being the Gaelic nickname of an eighteenth-century Highland outlaw called Robert MacGregor.

'We want more about our incredible Balinese Princess', British papers cried. And Marianne and Ratu obliged, relaying what one described as 'the amazing details of their insatiable sex life' and how they made love for six hours a night 'in 21 positions'.

Inspired by the Mick Jagger ceremonial wedding, I followed Ratu's trail through his earlier years in Bali, eager to confirm whether or not he was the esteemed Prince he claimed to be. There were many 'ho-ho-hos' among a group of friends I found in a cafe in Legian. It was time to find anyone related to the real king. While the last king had died in 1978, I learned that he had a son, his first-born, living on the north of the island, possibly in the town of Singaraja, although no-one seemed to know exactly where.

I rented a car and headed to the northern coast, located beside the Bali Sea. From Kuta it was about a three-hour drive, passing through the picturesque centre of the island, where life in the villages was far more relaxed than the chaos of the south. The centre rises up into a mountain range before the road drops down to Singaraja. Unlike Kuta, there were few tourists around.

Two hours of inquiries led me to a carved wooden door where I was told the old king's son lived. I pushed it open and found myself in a small courtyard. A tall, attractive Western woman approached, introducing herself as the German wife of the king's son, Dr Anak Agum Udayana. Eventually, he came out of the house, a middle-aged man with a welcoming smile. He and his wife offered me tea and looked questioningly at me for the reason I was there. When I told them the story of Ratu's marriage, Dr Udayana threw his head back, shaking it as he looked skywards.

'Oh dear,' he said. 'I am, of course, the real prince, so obviously Ratu has assumed my identity. I would be the real claimant to the throne – if there was a throne. He's a very distant relative and he certainly doesn't own eight palaces. As you can see, not even I live in a palace because most of them have fallen into disrepair. In fact, the palace that belonged to my father, the king, is now used as the town library and to house government departments.'

Dr Adayana shook his head again when I showed him photos of the wedding ceremony. 'That crown the young lady is wearing is what dancers wear when they put on a show. I can assure you that despite what she has been told, it is not a princess's crown and it is not made of solid gold. I am sorry to have to disappoint this young lady, but she has absolutely no standing as a Balinese princess. But if she wants to live in a palace, she could always make arrangements to stay in our town library.'

One big mystery remained. With the last king dead and not even his eldest son being able to step forward to claim the ruling position because Bali had been part of the Indonesian republic for the past 48 years, who were the king and queen who attended Marianne and Ratu's wedding? Had she been duped, or did she just misunderstand that two of Ratu's friends had agreed to act as stand-ins for the grand royal wedding that never was?

Away from the choking fumes of motor scooters, Bali evokes romance and romance can inspire imagination as wide as the ocean. While Marianne's love match had been struck in the US, once back in Ratu's territory she wanted to believe in all that he offered. But in the end, it was just a fairy tale.

CHAPTER TEN

AIRPORT DRAMA
- AND A CURIOUS CONFESSION

It is late afternoon in Bali airport in mid-July, 2017. Hundreds of passengers linger in the long walkways leading to the various departure gates from where they'll head off to their various countries. Most are suntanned, many carry souvenirs from their vacations. Children run about with Balinese-style braided hair. Some travellers decide to have a snack, even though they'll be eating again on the plane – if they don't decide to start sleeping as soon as they've taken off.

They are scenes that are familiar to airport staff around the world. Except that on this particular night, something different began to play out.

Australian Greg Butler was angry. Other passengers who glanced his way could see trouble in his face and stepped aside as he hurried along in his blue T-shirt and black shorts. The 46-year-old, who had caused problems on a flight, two days before, alarmed passengers as he shouted 'Corrupt…rude!' a number of times. Then he clambered over the wooden top of a glass barrier and threatened to jump to the second floor, 25 metres below. He clung on to the rail as security staff begged him to climb back over the barrier.

The pleas went on for more than an hour – officials worried that if they got too close Butler would carry out his threat and jump. Then at 6.18 pm Austrian tourist Erol Buyuk decided to help out. He told Butler to relax; that he just wanted to have a chat. Leaning casually on the rail, about a metre from the troubled man, Mr Buyuk told Butler that he wasn't alone with problems.

'All the people here have problems,' he told the Australian. 'I have more problems than you. My wife is here, we had our honeymoon here and look at my wife; she is crying. I have problems, but I am happy, we are happy and it is not correct what you do here.'

Eventually, with Mr Buyuk's help, security staff were able to grab Butler and haul him back over the glass barrier amid shouts and cheers from the other passengers.

'I never intended to jump,' he later told reporters. 'I didn't want to. I was standing on the edge. Would you jump?'

So, what was it all about? 'I wanted to point out corruption,' he said. 'It was to show up corrupt government officials.' It wasn't apparent which government he was referring to.

'I wanted to bring attention to certain situations regarding government officials and that's why I thought I could do it.'

Two days earlier Butler had caused the cancellation of an Air Asia flight from Bali to Kuala Lumpur when, just as the flight was about to take off, he jumped up from his seat, knocked on the cockpit door and said someone wanted to kill him. The pilot decided to return to the apron for safety reasons. Passengers were not amused. They had to spend the night in Kuta before taking another flight.

Butler was kept at the airport, where he was checked over by officials and doctors. Arie Ahsanurrohin, a senior communications official, said that it had been concluded that Butler had psychological problems because antidepressant medication was found in his bag. Following his investigation, he was left at the airport – and off he went to the barrier and climbed over.

This time he was sent to Sanglah Hospital to calm down. Police said he would not be charged because he had not committed a crime. Fortunately for him, he did not end up in Kerobokan Prison as another foreign statistic.

Some are there for life, expecting to die in captivity. Some await death by firing squad. Others serve out a time limit before they are free. The mental strength of each and every one can have an effect on how they survive each day. Heather Mack, the body in the suitcase killer – a phrase I adopted first when the hideous murder came to light – showed varying degrees of madness and calm.

She was able to communicate at times with Tommy Schaefer at the 'border' between the men's and women's blocks, but word was beginning to leak out that he was taking drugs from among the ample supply available within the prison. He talked of hating Heather because he had heard that she was flirting through the fence with male prisoners but also because she had reportedly started a lesbian relationship with two of the women who shared her cell.

As the months went by baby Stella had become the star of the cell. Far from earlier despising the thought of a young baby being in there with them and keeping them awake at night, Heather's cellmates now adored the child who they said helped to make their days more pleasurable.

Then came a new and totally unexpected drama. In October 2016 Schaefer, by then 23, wrote a six-page letter to friends in which he discussed the crime for the first time. And he accused Heather of spending all the 'sustenance' money – it was being provided to her from her murdered mother's estate by decree of a US judge – on drinks and drugs in her cell.

'She does all of this while having sex with women while my daughter is next to her,' he said in the letter. He also claimed that Heather was planning to make a film about the murder with a close friend of Sheila's.

There was further drama to be played out and it was a film, in a way. Heather uploaded three videos on YouTube – an example of how easy it was for prisoners to communicate to the outside world – remorselessly confessing to murdering her mother and getting Schaefer to force the body into the suitcase. Looking spaced out as she spoke to the camera in a blue top, one eye even looking bruised, Heather told the world that she had concocted the murder after learning that her mother was responsible for her jazz musician father's death in Greece in 2006. This, she said, was a video that she needed to make because 'I don't want to live in a lie anymore.' She claimed that she had asked Schaefer in the US to find somebody to kill her mother for $50,000 and he had said 'No'.

'I killed her myself and then I told Tommy that if he did not help me clean the room and get rid of the body, that I would tell the police that he did it, that I would pay money to get him arrested.'

She fought back tears as she said she regretted dragging Tommy, who was 'innocent', into her revenge plot, but added she felt no remorse for the murder.

'I don't regret killing my mother and as evil as that may sound, that's my reality,' she said.

It had been two weeks before she and her mother had set off for their vacation in Bali that she claimed she had learned that her mother had killed her father, she said. 'When I was ten, my mother killed my father in a hotel in Athens, Greece. Two weeks before I came to Bali, I found out that she killed my father and I made it up in my heart, in my mind, my soul, in my blood, in the oxygen running through my body, that I wanted to kill my mother. I got this whole new savage idea in my head that I wanted to kill her in a hotel room because she had killed my father in a hotel room.'

It was after she had supposedly learned this, she went on, that she had begun framing Schaefer by texting herself from his phone while he slept, to make it appear that he was discussing details of the murder. She had then deleted the exchanges before he saw them, she claimed.

Next, she said, she had booked him to join her on the holiday by using her mother's credit card. After the murder, she said she had coerced Schaefer to stuff the body in the suitcase, but up to then he had had no involvement in the actual killing, she claimed. While he had later confessed in court that he had killed Sheila in self-defence, Heather claimed in the video that she had forced him to lie for her.

'I trapped him here and that is what I regret. I regret being selfish. I regret trapping an innocent person into this because it was my battle, my mother, it was my father. I'm sorry to Tommy Schaefer for trapping him.' She further claimed that she and her lawyers had forced Schaefer in court to follow their lead, convincing him to confess to the murder so that she would not be cut off from the more than a million dollars she stood to inherit. 'I'm still entitled to the money and therefore I can pay the lawyers more,' she said, referring to an alleged courtroom plan to be found innocent of the murder.

'So, we told Tommy together, my lawyers and I, that if he didn't take the blame in the court, that he would get the death penalty. So, he lied in court because of me. My motivation for doing this was myself.'

Heather also maintained in the video that Schaefer's cousin Robert Bibbs, who had pleaded guilty in the US to helping in the plot to kill Sheila, was innocent. 'I don't even know how he got involved in this or why the FBI involved him because he had absolutely nothing to do with any of it,' she said. 'He's innocent. I don't know if he wanted to sell a better story or what the FBI was on, but Tommy and Robert are innocent. I'm not.'

Before signing off from the astonishing video, Heather added in a message aimed at Schaefer that she was sorry and that she loved him. 'I'm sorry you won't be able to get a job, I'm sorry everybody thinks that you're some crazy killer. This is the truth and whoever is watching this, don't hate Tommy. He's innocent. I'm not…I love you Tommy.'

Heather's claim that Sheila had murdered her father, James Mack, was ludicrous as obituaries had recorded his death was from a pulmonary embolism. But there was something more about the video. Grammatically, it seemed too 'perfect', such as the phrase, 'So we told Tommy together, my lawyers and I…'

Then, a few days later, on 8 February 2017, came the 'truth' – or Heather's version of it.

For she claimed that the video was false, had been made more than a year previously and she had been pressured into making it and what to say. Her boyfriend, she said, had written it for her and had passed it to her to read to the camera.

'I have no idea how this ended up on YouTube,' she told Kerobokan prison officials – and her Bali lawyers said in a statement that she was denying the contents.

Her legal representative, Mr Yulius Seran, said the contents of the video were fake by design and recorded under pressure about 12 months earlier.

'Tommy Schaefer has written the scenario of confession…have in mind at the time when the video was made, around June 11 2016. Heather Mack put a handwritten letter from Tommy in front of her to be read,' said Mr Seran.

Heather, he said, had not uploaded the video. Other parties, said Mr Seran, had created an account with the name Heather Mack in order to create the illusion that it was her doing.

'Heather Mack is a victim of such a fake video and allegedly there is the motivation behind the video published on the YouTube page to affect the ongoing trial in Chicago [of Schaefer's cousin] as well as efforts to interfere the process of transition of Stella's guardianship.'

Heather faced denial of privileges in the prison if it could be proved she had uploaded the video, especially as phones and use of the internet are banned in the jail. But it appeared later that officials were in agreement she had not known about that the recording had been uploaded.

There was no doubt that she had faced a camera and spoken the words. The suspected black eye she appeared to be showing might have had something to do with her agreeing to read the 'confession'.

CHAPTER ELEVEN

CASANOVAS AND SCHOOLIES

Beside the wall separating Kuta Beach from the one-way road, close to a toilet block, there's a lady with a hose pipe who will wash the sand off your feet if you've got anything more sophisticated than a pair of flip-flops to put on. She and her friends at other foot-washing 'stations' don't ask for much, but they make enough to get them through another day.

Close by are other locals who stand to make much more money if they play their cards right. They are fit, muscular, bronzed young men whose eyes skim the beaches and the female tourists who stretch out with sun-oiled skin, lapping up the warmth and occasionally getting up to run to the sea to cool down. If there's no obvious boyfriend in sight and the woman appears to be alone, a local man might try an approach, nothing heavy, just a hello, can I sit down here, where are you from. If he's lucky she won't give him the brush off and if he's really, really, lucky she might agree to go for a drink or a bite to eat with him later that day.

Such young men don't like being referred to as gigolos or, Kuta Cowboys – descriptions that were from another time, before the police rounded up more than 20 of them a few years ago and warned them they were giving Bali and Indonesia in general a bad image. They simply had to stop flirting with the tourists.

But sex is sex and officialdom can't crush it, otherwise world-wide prostitution wouldn't be known as the planet's oldest profession. It is, naturally, illegal in Indonesia, but the young men who sit on the sea wall or have a game of beach football before hitting the nightclubs insist that if they end up in bed with a tourist it's love and love alone. A two-way street. No prostitution here, officer. This lady loves me.

'No, don't call us gigolos,' says 22-year-old DannyBoy, emerging from a convenience store near the beach with a cold cola to sit at one of the outdoors wooden tables. 'If a woman want to pay us with money or gifts, it's up to her. We just make ourselves available to meet her needs. Don't think that respectable-looking women, a bit on the wealthy side, aren't interested in the likes of me. They leave their country, wherever, for a holiday and all the time they're hoping they'll find romance. It's a fact of life. Maybe they'll have a good time with me or one of my friends – and maybe I'll have a good time if she takes me out to dinner and we have good sex at the end of the day. I don't ask for money and I don't expect it. I just want to have fun like she does.'

The young men who meet the needs of lonely or adventurous tourists speak English as well as their native Indonesian, but many have also learned to hold a basic conversation in several languages, a reflection on the number of international tourists they have entertained.

'The secret is for them to take me back to their hotel,' says Kadek, a 26-year-old Java man who has lived in Bali for 12 years, finding menial work in a scooter repair shop and helping in a kitchen restaurant. 'I could never take a tourist back to where I live – a small room I share with three other guys. Some of the women I've dated have stayed at the top hotels, which could be a problem if you don't know how to play the game. The best hotels have security guards who look out for their wealthy guests being in the company of a local man and there have been times when I've been stopped. But there are always ways of getting to their room – by invitation, of course.'

The men, who continue to insist they are not gigolos, have turned to tourists young and old because there's often very little work around and, as one says, 'You can get hungry if you spend the day surfing. You need the friendship of a woman in the hope she'll buy you a meal – just as she needs the friendship of a man to satisfy her sexual needs.'

Who are these women who turn to strangers in Bali, when in their own countries they wouldn't entertain the idea of having sex without romantic foreplay?

As with so many tourists, there is something about Bali where caution is thrown to the wind. It is, says one British woman, a mother of two adult children who wanted to be known only as 'Monica from near Manchester', 'a feeling of freedom, of getting away from all the troubles you have at home and embracing a new environment, making new friends, in fact making the most of every minute you have and perhaps opening the door to a whole new life.' Pointedly, she adds, 'I had a short relationship with a local boy. I just wanted to be understood and he was happy to listen. I could tell him things about all my troubles and there was no danger of him gossiping, like they would back in the UK. In Bali, I was anonymous. I might meet up with him again. I don't know…haven't seen him for a few days.'

It's not just Western women who allow themselves to be chatted up by handsome young Balinese men. Asians, Japanese and Koreans in particular, have been drawn to the formerly-named Kuta Cowboys. In 2014 a Japanese magazine reported that the country's young women were heading to Bali because they wanted to meet gigolos. More than meet them, said the magazine, they were willing to fork out 584,000 rupiah ($55), a lot of money for a Balinese, to be accompanied for a full day, although that day might come with 'extras'.

Claiming that there were more than 200 gigolos working in Bali that were known of, although there were likely to be many more, the magazine said that it was 'quite common for the Japanese woman to ask the beach boy to do a very exotic massage from top to bottom. Then at some point during that massage the woman asks how much it's going to cost for the 'full' service. The article said that many gigolos 'actually take the time to get special training on how to satisfy a woman. These gigolos really are looking for repeat business and with the disposable income of these Japanese women on the rise the demand is likely to continue to grow, especially as the practice becomes more open and awareness increases.'

The fact that the word 'gigolo' is whispered these days, rather than casually and openly referred to along the beachfront, is mainly due to a documentary *Cowboys in Paradise*, made by Singapore-based writer and director Amit Virmani, whose film about the 'beach boys' and the women who fell for them went viral in 2010. The film resulted in 28 voyeurs accused of selling sex to tourists being rounded up amid the fears of tourism officials that the documentary could impact Bali's image as a family destination.

'Such cowboys have been a fixture on Bali's beaches for some time but hadn't attracted much attention until now,' said the chief of the island's tourism board, Ida Bagus Ngurah Wijaya. 'The film is over the top and only focuses on this group of people on the beach, but that's not what Bali is about. If the film is shown to the world, Bali's image will be tarnished.

I hope the authorities will get rid of these cowboys because they're of no benefit to us.'

Meanwhile the chief of security on Kuta Beach, I Gusti Ngurah Tresna, said the documentary ran counter to the authorities' preferred image of Bali as a world-class destination combining unique Hindu culture and history with the famous beaches and surfing areas. 'All this while we've been selling our beautiful waves, sunsets, turtles, culture and nature conservation and suddenly now we're seen to be selling gigolos? Such films are really harmful to our image.' Mr Tresna added that 'it's like prostitution which is hard to prove because the foreign women may be willing partners too.'

Defending his documentary, filmmaker Virmani said many people scoffed at the need to distinguish between cowboys and gigolos, but he saw the distinction. 'The cowboys are the most visible face of Bali's male sex trade, but they're not sex workers,' he insisted.

Despite the earlier row arising from the film, the gigolos, the cowboys, the hunters – whatever name they go by – the young Balinese men who hope to hook up with a foreign woman are still there on the beach and along the beachfront. Their ultimate aim is not just a holiday romance – the love being appreciated more by the women than by themselves, many will admit – but the hope that they will strike it lucky and be offered a trip back to the woman's home country. And after that? Marriage. And a brand new life with all its prospects, a sharp comparison with the uncertain future that awaits them in Bali.

• • •

The women who find real or make-believe romance in Bali, singularly, in pairs, perhaps with a few friends, are a stark contrast to another group who touch down each year knowing exactly what lies ahead. They are 'the schoolies', 6000 school leavers from Australia who band together to 'invade' Bali with the sole purpose of having the time of their young lives. Being 4620 kilometres from home, this is where they will let their hair down without parental control. In most cases it will just be wild, crazy fun, maybe too much alcohol, a fist thrown here and there, but no serious damage is caused. But what the Balinese see – although they have become used to it all in recent years – is outrageous Western decadence, behaviour that clashes with their own peaceful culture.

Yet there are elements among the Balinese themselves who are ready for the teenagers; ready, that is, to offer them marijuana, ice, cocaine, ecstasy and magic mushrooms. The boys have frequently been targeted with offers of Viagra, some pills being fakes. Fortunately, the warnings that have preceded them have resulted in many schoolies now refusing to buy, but a few fall victim to the temptation and end up relying on their friends to help them get home at the end of the night. The drug sellers risk long prison sentences, but usually they work from the dark and are not easily tracked down and caught. In any case, the word on the streets is that the pushers are in cohorts with the police – sell the drugs, 'shop' the buyer, put the narcotics back in circulation.

The Balinese themselves, and expatriate business owners, do try to separate schoolies from drugs. The manager of the Bounty Hotel, popular among the young arrivals, personally issued a warning to his guests to stay clear not only of drugs offered in the street but to stay away from cocktails that are sold cheaply – they have been known to drive teenagers crazy. One teenager who drank a large amount of 'jungle juice' containing methanol lost his vision and had to be airlifted off the island to a hospital in northern Australia.

Because alcohol is expensive in Muslim Indonesia, high prices are also charged in Bali for genuine spirits. So young people learning that tequila can be bought at a fraction of the 'regular' price are warned to be very suspicious and avoid the cheap local version. In particular an Indonesian drink called arrack can be particularly dangerous because it can contain dangerous levels of methanol.

On any night during the schoolies invasion in Kuta, Legian and Seminyak there is hedonistic madness in the air: shrieks of laughter from the girls, drunken roars from the boys, inside and outside nightclubs such as the SC Bar, the Bounty and The Engine Room. They weave through the traffic on their rented scooters, many ignoring the compulsory helmet rules. But it's not just the young who take the risks. Adults, too, pour the drinks down and then try to ride home to their hotels. There are no roadside breath tests as such, although police might randomly pull someone over to check their licence.

For a while a few years ago, some police were pulling a scam, demanding to see an international driver's licence. Facing a fine, an officer would suggest a European could avoid a big fine by paying on the spot there and then. The money went into the back pocket. Enlightened about this, the authorities cracked down on such activities, although there have been more recent reports of the scam being pulled from time to time.

The drug dealers pull their own kind of swindle, selling white powder to naive teenagers who believe they and their friends can get high on the 'bargain' cocaine they have purchased, only to find it's talcum powder. In 2016 Jamie Murphy, a teenager from Perth, was arrested by police who suspected he was in possession of cocaine, but he ended up being thankful that he had been conned because tests revealed that his 'cocaine' was paracetamol. An investigation by News Corporation discovered another scam in which a dealer does a high-five with the drugs in his hand in an effort to get it into a schoolie's hand, after which they demand money. This was drug-pushing in the extreme.

Chloe Withers, a Victorian teenager, told News that they had to constantly refuse drugs as they moved around the streets of Kuta. 'You just have to walk away from them and they won't keep hassling you.' She questioned the stupidity of buying drugs in a country which had harsh narcotics laws and was internationally known for jailing, and in some cases executing, foreigners caught with drugs.

Even so, the drugs are there for the taking, with prices varying depending on who's selling. But on average ecstasy costs about $20 for a single pill while five grams of marijuana – ganja – is on offer for $100. Aside from the pushers, an equally sinister group moves among the crowds of partying teenagers – thieves. Their targets are handbags, purses, mobile phones, anything that can be grabbed while the owner is temporarily – and it can be just a few seconds – immersed in the loud music and disco lights. One mobile phone thief was caught by security guards and was given a severe beating.

There is another group who add to the risks taken by teenagers as they pour back the alcohol. 'Toolies', the older men who fly in to Bali from around the world with the sole purpose of picking up a reveller for sex, are as morally dangerous as the pushers. Some are old enough to be fathers of the women they target in the clubs, moving in to dance with them but then starting to grope. One report told of an older Russian man climbing onto a podium to dance with the girls, but then he began touching them inappropriately, to the disgust of others. Creepy, disgusting, dirty; they were words that young women used for the older men who slithered in around them in the crowded clubs. But one self-described toolie claimed that the 'talent' was worth visiting the Bali clubs for.

'There are a lot of out of control girls out because they have never been clubbing before. They have no experience with all of this. They are easy as; you can pick them up, no worries.' He always tried to take them back to their hotel 'so they don't know where I stay'.

It is dawn on Kuta Beach. The sun is yet to beam down, move across the sky and, 12 hours later, present one of the magnificent sunsets that the beach is famous for. But for now, for at least a dozen or more revellers, the sands provide a bed. They've had too much to drink the night before and have flopped down on the beach, soon to wake to killer headaches from the cheap drinks they've consumed; or they've met someone in a club and sex on the beach has become a natural progression.

By the time the sun has also started to wake, it's time for regrets…

CHAPTER TWELVE

'NEVER, EVER, TAKE THE BALINESE FOR GRANTED'

It was in the late 1980s and I was sitting with Andre in a cafe known to the locals as 'the pudding shop', a ten-minute walk from Kuta beachfront. It had a tiered seating arrangement and a great atmosphere, earning its nickname from the old hippies who remembered the cheap cake and tea shops of Turkey, Iran and Afghanistan, when those countries posed no danger for adventurous wanderers. Andre was a French photographer living in Bali, mostly shooting picturesque photos for postcards – and yes, he made a good living out of it.

Andre knew quite a bit about the ins and outs of living on the holiday island. He'd seen enough people coming and going to be in a position to give what was prophetic advice for those who were to follow.

'Come to Bali and enjoy yourself,' he said, fiddling with his old Leica film camera, a hint, perhaps, that he wanted to stay in the past. 'Swim in the hotel pool, order a mango juice, jump in the sea, have fun in the nightclubs, ride around the island, return the smile of locals, but never, ever, take them for granted. Never, ever, assume the police are naive. Never, ever big-note yourself or be rude. Never, ever, think: "These people are pretty backward; I can get away with whatever I like." Because the tables will turn and you'll regret it.'

I could have spoken to a psychologist or sociologist to find reasons for tourists behaving differently to the way they would act at home once they've touched down in Bali, or any other exotic location come to that, but I wanted to hear it from a 'street level' observer like 52-year-old Andre.

'It's like I said. They think they can get away with it. They think they're superior. They think that because the way of life here might be more simple, it's a case of anything goes. It's the heat, it's the beer, it's the absence of any visible form of strict authority. Tourists might come from a country where there are laws everywhere but in Bali they gain the impression that nobody cares if you do something wrong. Big mistake to think that.'

July 2017. An unlucky month for some Westerners in Bali with the arrest of an American armed robber and the deaths of three tourists.

> He's been here a long time and has a small baby, so I figure he has to have hit very desperate times to be committing a crime of this nature. It is reported elsewhere that he told police he came here a wealthy man and had fallen on hard times.
>
> He is someone I know and am saddened that he is in this situation though I cannot condone what he has done. I wish he had at least asked me for a loaner. I might not have loads of cash floating around but I could have paid for some baby formula and diapers.

The writer on an expatriate website was referring to Paul Hoffman, a 57-year-old American from New York who had just been sent to jail for 20 months for, astonishingly, going around to convenience stores and threatening staff with a knife and demanding money and bottles of whisky before riding away on a motor scooter. The word around town was that Hoffman, who had been living in Sanur, really had hit bad times and was having trouble making ends meet.

The first of what was to be eight store robberies was in February 2017 when he selected a bottle of water from the fridge in a shop then pulled out the knife when the cashier opened the money drawer. He took 8.7 million rupiah ($785) along with two bottles of whisky, Black Label and Red Label.

A day later, he struck at another store but this time he escaped with just 176,000 rupiah ($15). Then, in Seminyak on 14 February he stole 800,000 rupiah ($72). He later hit another convenience store in Seminyak, escaping with 11 million rupiah ($990).

His run of robberies continued and it seemed that, from their pattern, he would eventually be caught, particularly as his sandy-haired features had been captured on CCTV. And caught he was. When he appeared in Denpasar Court on 5 July, charged with just four of what were allegedly at least eight offences, prosecutors asked for him to be sent to prison for two and a half years. It was looking bad for Hoffman after Chief Justice Ginarsa noted that 'the defendant was proven convincingly and legally guilty of theft by violence or by threat of violence against others.'

But the judge dismissed the request for a long jail sentence, imposing the 20-month term and saying he had been impressed with Hoffman's politeness and the fact that he had been helpful during police investigations. A court official said it might have also been regarded that Hoffman's activities, when he must have known he would be caught, were a cry for help.

Later in July came the discovery of the bodies of three Western men in separate incidents.

On 10 July at 1.30 pm the body of 43-year-old English psychologist Scott Mynors was found in his rented accommodation in Sanur. The cause of death for the man, who was head of the Loud Waters Mineral Company, was not immediately confirmed but police said they suspected he had died from a heart attack after consuming alcohol and prescription drugs. According to local media, police found two bottles of rum, nutritional supplements and a drug used to treat agitation and anxiety near his body.

Twelve days later Peter Machtelinckx, a 57-year-old Belgian, jumped to his death from the second floor of a villa in Bali's Gianyar Regency. Cleaning staff found his body on a walkway at 6.20 am. He had sustained massive head injuries and could not be saved.

Police said that Mr Machtelinckx had been plagued by an unpaid debt in Belgium of two million euros, along with a number of family problems.

On that very same Saturday morning of 22 July, following an evening of beer drinking with his family and friends in a hotel in East Bali, the body of 53-year-old New Zealand tourist David Fraser was found at the mouth of a river. According to witnesses, his wife Manren had gone back to their room the previous evening, leaving her husband at the bar with friends. When she awoke in the early hours and realised her husband had not returned, she went looking for him without success.

At 6.50 that morning a hotel worker discovered Mr Fraser's body in the estuary. Police found no signs of a struggle or violence and there were no other obvious signs of death. But whatever the cause – heart attack, drowning or other – there is no official category that would sum up all fatalities: tragedy in Bali.

Families, friends and individuals, they leave their homes from around the world to fly to Indonesia's exotic location seeking relaxation, adventure, cultural education, romance, perhaps a business opportunity. But sadly, dozens each year fail to make the return journey; most have died on the roads, others have ended up in jail. And there are some who are so badly injured in accidents that they have to be medically evacuated, their futures crippled, literally.

Riding a scooter without a helmet looks good, feels good. At least that's what thousands of tourists believe each year when they hire a bike. They zap around Kuta, the guys in their Bintang Beer sleeveless vests, girlfriends clinging on behind, summer dresses flailing, bronzed legs on display. Death, maiming or a bad scarring could be minutes, even seconds away. The metallic bang as a bike hits a car, a scream, the crack of broken bones, the gushing of blood; no-one imagines that such a scene could involve them. Right then the freedom is just grand – so much better than having to obey the strict road rules of their home country.

It's easy enough for a tourist to hire a scooter, even if they've never ridden one before. The machine might have familiar controls but a certain skill is required to actually ride it on the narrow, crowded roads of Bali. Road rules that apply in the UK, the US, Australia, New Zealand, for example don't apply in Bali. A stop sign – at least those that exist – means 'keep going, maybe a little more slowly' to a local. Riding in the jam-packed roads requires an awareness of what's in front, at each side and behind at all times. There's no comfort zone. Potential death is a constant. Zig-zagging in and out of the traffic is fun for the newcomer who has embraced the feeling of anything goes in a land of 'lawlessness' – until something goes wrong and the next minute the bike is down, the tourist is down and he or she is being run over by all who follow. Recent reports show that some 150 tourists are involved in road accidents in Bali every year, the age range being from 17 to 30. There's one other reason for tourists to be very careful when riding; if they're involved in an accident the chances are that they will be blamed for the cause, even if they're innocent.

So, road accidents will bring about a swift end to a dream holiday, and so too will alcohol-fuelled violence. Schoolies who have drunk too much have found out to their detriment that trading blows can result in serious injury, particularly if the opponent happens to be a local who will quickly be aided by other Balinese. And even if a night in the clubs passes without incident, getting onto a scooter while intoxicated, either as the rider or passenger, can be fatal.

Over a period of a year up to April 2017, three Australians died in scooter accidents, with many others being seriously injured. Australia's Department of Foreign Affairs makes a special point on its website about the dangers of riding a scooter, emphasising that a number of foreigners have been killed or seriously injured in tourist areas. 'In the event of an accident, it will often be assumed that the foreigner is at fault and they will be expected to make financial restitution to all other parties…wear and ensure your passenger wears, a correctly fastened and approved helmet.'

Among the numerous deaths in road accidents in recent years, there was the fatal accident involving adventure-seeking Simon Bonnici. Bali was the first leg of a six-month trip that would have taken in the US and Mexico. He was an experienced rider, as his restored Harley-Davidson motor cycle back at home revealed, but the dangers of travelling on a motorbike in Bali brought a tragic end to his life on the road.

Two other deaths followed in 2016 with Australian Lochie Connaughton dying when he lost control of a scooter in Kuta in an accident that, on the face of it, should never have happened. He was riding out of the basement of a Kuta hotel when he lost control. A month later 42-year-old firefighter Adrian Newton was killed when police said his motorbike collided with a garbage truck in Kuta.

In April 2017, came the death of 27-year-old tourist Ella Knights, who fell from a scooter in North Kuta. She was found by a passer-by lying face down in the gutter, a Honda scooter on its side nearby with its engine still running. *The Sydney Morning Herald*, looking back on her life, recalled that earlier that month she had travelled to Bali where she posted images of lying on the beach with friends, eating healthy food and practising yoga. When a friend asked when she would be returning home, she jokingly responded, 'Well, right now I'm trying for never, ha ha.' Later, in what turned out to be a chilling message, she posted a photo of herself riding on the back of a scooter in Bali declaring, 'Sorry mum #nohelmet.'

Badung Precinct Traffic Police Chief Raka Wiratma revealed that the distance between Ella and the bike was around two metres. 'According to several witnesses she was riding the bike alone and not wearing a helmet.

We suspect the victim was out of control.' Hospital staff suggested later that Ella had suffered bruises and wounds all over her face, as well as injuries to other parts of her body. It was a tragic end to a wholesome life; Ella, documenting her travels on Instagram, revealed she had spent time in India learning yoga and had become a qualified yoga teacher.

Recent statistics show that 35 foreigners died in Bali over the 12-month period to May 2016, although they were not all the result of accidents or violence. Most died from heart attacks and pre-existing illnesses, but many 'incidents' simply go unreported, with tourists who escaped a near-death or very frightening experience, such as a mugging or rape, not wanting to become caught up in a complex legal system far from home.

'Let's be straight, most fatalities that come to me are the result of natural causes,' says Dr Dudut Rustyadi, head mortician at Sanglah Hospital. 'You only hear about the young ones when people talk about tourism, but the fact is many elderly people come here to relax in the evening of their lives, so it's not surprising that some die here.'

But of course, there are the road accident victims with fatal head injuries because they haven't been wearing a helmet or the helmet is sub-standard, having been purchased from a roadside kiosk for as little as $10. The helmets might look the part but when it comes to protecting a skull they are totally useless. Even helmets that pass the safety test are of little use if they are not worn properly, securely strapped on.

Retired engineer John Bourke, 63, was enjoying his life in his villa not far from Kerobokan prison. He had moved to Bali from Darwin, northern Australia, some ten years earlier to spend the rest of his days on the holiday island, but he could never have imagined that his death would come from a savage beating in a home invasion in May 2016. Curiously, he had recently asked a friend to care for his dog 'in case anything happens to me'. He had been attacked just two weeks earlier, but the second assault was brutal and fatal. The floor of his home was covered in pools of blood when he was found.

Nothing appeared to have been taken from the villa and there were suggestions his beating was the result of a property dispute. Mr Bourke did not die immediately, but for the next few days he lay critically injured in hospital as doctors worked to reduce swelling around his brain. Police waited at his bedside, hoping that he would come out of a coma and tell them about his attacker or attackers, but he passed away without regaining consciousness. Polce Fanggidae, who had been staying in the villa at the time of the attack, told police that he had found John Bourke lying in a pool of blood after hearing noises during the night.

'When I was asleep, around 1.30 am, I heard noises but I didn't think anything of it and went back to sleep,' he told the *Brisbane Times*. 'By 4.30 am I heard louder noises. When John didn't answer, I looked down from the second floor and saw him in the living room, covered in blood. There were trails of blood from his room to the living room. I think he was expecting trouble because he asked me three days ago take care of his dog in case something happened to him. He cared a lot about the dog.'

Another friend, Brandon Ingram, said the retiree had been attacked with a weapon similar to a machete, while a neighbour suggested that an earlier assault inside the villa nearly two weeks previously might have been a failed attempt on his life. On that occasion, his dog had alerted him when an intruder armed with a wooden club had broken into the house. 'A guy came into the villa and beat John, but he managed to defend himself and the assailant fled,' said the neighbour.

Death can come to tourists when they are doing nothing more dangerous than walking along a beach. It happened to two visitors, from Hong Kong and Singapore, who were dragged out to sea when huge waves swept over them at Padang Galak Beach in Sanur in June 2016. Their deaths from the mountainous waves that hit Bali that month came following the deaths of five people, including a woman who was on honeymoon, who was dragged out to sea.

The tourists had flown to Bali for a dream holiday, but many ended up posting messages on social media about the terrifying sea conditions. 'Dude, where's my beach?' one tourist asked. 'Global warming working its charms.' Another wrote, 'King tide has hit Seminyak too! Pool usually has a huge beach in front of it. Now it has a beach *in* it!'

Then there are the incidents at sea, with lives being lost due to poor maintenance of tourist boats or bad decisions being made to set off in rough weather. Bali is one of the main launching places for a trip to other islands in the region, such as Lombok, the Gili Islands group or, further afield, Komodo island, home, with other islands nearby, to the fierce dragon.

In September 2016 a woman and a young girl were killed and several other tourists were injured when a speedboat on a $30-a-head ride from Sanur to the Gili Islands burst into flames when a fuel container exploded, the blast tearing through the passenger cabin, blowing out windows and throwing tourists out of their seats. An Austrian woman and a 12-year-old Austrian girl were killed. An Italian woman lost both her legs below the knee.

The terrifying experience involved 13 British travellers, four French, four Italians, four Austrians and two each from Germany, Ireland, Holland, Spain and Portugal – the passenger list revealing just how many varying foreign visitors can be found in all areas of Bali. The incident also left the reputation of the island's tour ships in tatters, following a series of disasters over the years.

Aside from hundreds of Indonesians dying in ferry mishaps, mostly caused by overcrowding, tourists have died or narrowly escaped death after problems with vessels plying the waters around Bali and other islands.

In August 2014 two British sisters, Katherine and Alice Ostojkic, who had based themselves in Bali, had to swim for eight hours to safety after a tour boat sank near Komodo Island.

Later Katherine, 21, and her 19-year-old sister told of sitting on the overturned semi-submerged hull of their tour boat after it was struck by rough seas. After realising their chances of being rescued were getting slimmer by the minute they had no option but to join eight fellow survivors in swimming to an island on the horizon.

In an email to their parents they wrote that, 'In case the embassy haven't contacted yet, we were involved in the Indonesian boat sinking but are fine, having swum to shore. The British embassy in Denpasar are helping us…'

The following day, 18 August 2014, Katherine wrote that everyone had been found and, summing up what happened, added:

> the boat sank in the middle of the night. We sat on its roof while it was semi-submerged for 10 hours, then swam for 8 hours to the shore before seeing the lights of some fishermen and getting them to pick us up.

Spent the night on an uninhabited active volcanic island with the fishermen who gave us food and water before we were taken back to a larger island.

As the varied incidents involving the tourist-crowded island reveal, some are lucky, others not.

CHAPTER THIRTEEN

'GANJA QUEEN'

Schapelle was in trouble and the fear in her startling blue eyes showed it. Within just 24 hours of her detention at the airport local media were describing her as the 'Ganja Queen'. But there was nothing queenly about the cell she was being held in at Kerobokan jail. And for each consecutive hearing as her case proceeded through the courts there was just chaos, with every seat in the public part of the courtroom jammed with curious locals and media.

At one stage, sitting before the panel of three judges as prosecutors and lawyers put their cases before the court, Schapelle's head turned to the gallery and she cried in despair, 'I need some help here.'

The first witness when the trial opened in January 2005 was Ngurah Winata, the customs officer who had ordered Schapelle to open the boogie board bag. As Schapelle, her eyes fixed on him, listened to his testimony through an interpreter, he told how she had opened a front pocket in the bag, instead of the main part, before she told him 'Nothing in there.'

But he said he had wanted the main flap opened, at which time Schapelle had simply said 'No.' When he asked her why, said Winata, she had replied 'I have some...' and, he said, she looked confused. He told of finding the flippers in the case when he opened it, and then he found the plastic bags, one inside the other, with the marijuana as well as the boogie board. She had, he said, then confessed that marijuana was in the plastic bags and she claimed she knew what it was because she smelled it when the main bag was opened.

'He's lying!' Schapelle cried, leaping to her feet. 'I opened the bag at the customs counter. He did not ask me. I opened it myself. I saw a plastic bag inside. It had been half opened.' And yes, she realised it was marijuana because of the smell.

The court heard Winata and a second officer deny that the bag had been opened after the airport X-ray machine had detected the drugs.

They also denied inspecting the drugs before zipping the bag shut again. The hearing boiled down to a situation of 'he said, she said, he did, she did'. But Schapelle pressed on with her claim that the bag had been unzipped and then zipped shut in a way that she never closed it.

In the early stages of the trial, Schapelle's defence team – Erwin Siregar, Haposan Sihombing, Lily Sri Rahaya Lubis and her assistant, Vasu Rasiah – made much of the way the boogie board case had been opened and closed, insisting there was evidence of interference. What became clear, too, was that the plastic bags, one inside the other, had not been tested for fingerprints, a critical manoeuvre. Schapelle told her lawyers to make it clear to the court that if fingerprint testing had taken place, they would not find hers on the plastic bags. No, the court heard, fingerprints had not been taken but eventually Senior Commissioner Bambang Sugiarto, director of Bali's narcotics bureau, promised to have the testing done. But as time was to reveal, it never was.

In any case, the lawyers' continual insistence that the plastic bags be tested became academic when, during Schapelle's second court appearance on 3 February, the internal bag with the drugs was handled by a number of court officials, including the customs officers, Prosecutor Ida Bagus Wiswantanu and even assistant judge I Gusti Lanang Dauh. Once again, however, in the vague hope that evidence in favour of Schapelle would be found, her lawyers pleaded for the fingerprinting to go ahead. Despite the critical need for the tests to be made – for Schapelle's guilt or innocence depended mostly on whether her prints were on the marijuana bag – Chief Judge Linton Sirat would only go so far as to say he would 'consider' ordering the tests.

While the handling of the boogie board bag and its contents proved to be a confusing issue, despite it being a matter of vital importance in Schapelle's defence, it emerged that officials at the airport had failed to weigh Schapelle's baggage. This was another critical point because her lawyers argued that if her luggage weighed more on arrival in Bali than it had when she first checked it in at Brisbane airport, it would be evidence that extra weight, the marijuana, had been added during transport.

Schapelle insisted that the bags be weighed, but this was not done, just as the fingerprinting had not been carried out. Working against her claims of innocence, too, was the fact that CCTV camera footage, which could have supported her account of what had happened at the airport, was not made available to her lawyers, and they also failed to obtain photos of the X-ray scanning of the boogie board bag because the machine was not set up to take any.

Back in Kerobokan, Schapelle wept frequently in her cell. But according to other prisoners who were released, her fellow inmates gave her great comfort, among them British drug mule Lindsay Sandiford, and others who had been convicted of importing, carrying or using large amounts of narcotics.

'I shouldn't be here. I'm just trying to be strong and I'm just lucky that I've got really good family and friends to help me get through,' she told a visitor. It was a message that she had put about whenever she had the opportunity and every word she had uttered, either in the court or when she was being led in and out, was followed by millions around the world who had debated her predicament – guilty or not guilty – in homes, bars and restaurants. There could not have been an adult in Australia, in particular, who did not know about the case, for cameras had been allowed into the courtroom and the TV channels obligingly met the demand for step-by-step coverage.

But Schapelle admitted that her lawyers had a tough fight ahead of them because the prosecution had outlined a basic premise: she had agreed the boogie board case was hers and the marijuana had been found inside, therefore the marijuana had to be hers. On 17 February the prosecution wound up its case. Now came the very hard part – the fight for Schapelle to be found not guilty, because if her defence failed she was looking at many years in jail.

A question arose, however, about the strength of her lawyers. Lily Lubis handled civil cases mostly and another of her team, Vasu Rasiah, was actually not a lawyer at all but a man involved in a property development business in Bali. He told reporters that he should be regarded as the case coordinator, a person believed to have been appointed by Lily Lubis.

From the start, Schapelle's team argued that she had no knowledge of the marijuana until it was found by customs officials. In fact, they proposed, she had become an unwitting drug courier for what was meant to have been a shipment of cannabis between Brisbane and Sydney. It meant, they said, that crooked airport baggage handlers had slipped the drugs into the boogie board case. But this was merely a claim – they were not able to provide any evidence of this.

Even so, the defence team looked to every angle, including having private meetings with Foreign Minister Alexander Downer. Prime Minister John Howard, when asked if the government could have any influence, said, 'We will do everything that we are properly and reasonably asked to do to see that any relevant evidence is presented.' It was all that he could say. He had to stop short of being seen to interfere with the laws of Indonesia, but in any case, Schapelle's sister, Mercedes, had no doubt she would be found not guilty.

'She's innocent so she'll be coming home,' Mercedes said outside the court.

Part way into Schapelle's defence case came a totally unexpected new player, mobile phone entrepreneur Ron Bakir, also known as Mad Ron. In what has been described as a Balinese soap opera, Bakir flew to Denpasar with his lawyer friend Robin Tampoe, who, in 2009, was to be struck off for boasting that he had invented a defence for Schapelle and had also disclosed confidential information about her family.

Mad Ron, a Lebanese-Australian, entered the case after his personal assistant urged him to look into Schapelle's predicament. He'd been following it closely and he had already concluded that there were more questions than answers surrounding the arrest and charging of a fellow Queenslander. He gained access to Schapelle in Kerobokan jail and told her of his total support. In a series of media interviews, he said he was going to prove that Schapelle was innocent. One factor that did arise as Schapelle's case for her defence wound on was where the marijuana had originated. If it had come from Queensland, the scales might weigh against Schapelle, but as it was, Indonesian police refused a request by the Australian Federal Police to have the source tested.

It was time for yet another unexpected player to enter the scene. 'Mad Ron' Bakir was accompanied by defence team coordinator Vasu Rasiah when he flew to Canberra to meet the Attorney-General, the Justice Minister and Australian Federal Police in the hope of persuading them to release a remand prisoner in Victoria's Port Phillip Prison. John Patrick Ford had earlier come forward to provide a statement about corrupt baggage handlers who shipped drugs through Australian airports. Schapelle reportedly broke down in tears when she heard of the new development in her fight. 'Oh my God,' she cried with relief.

It was on 29 March 2005, that Ford, who had been on remand in Australia on unconnected matters, sat before the three judges as Schapelle prepared to listen to words that could lead to her freedom. His own appearance in Bali did not mean he was a free man – on his arrival he had been locked in a police cell where he unhappily spent the night before his appointment with the court.

During two hours of testimony he told of conversations he had heard in prison between two inmates called 'Terry' and 'Paul' – he didn't know their surnames – six months earlier. He said he had heard them laughing because cannabis belonging to a man called Ronnie had gone missing while being transport from Brisbane airport to Sydney and had ended up in Indonesia. The joke was, said Ford, that somebody had been caught for it and was going to do time for it. The court was left in no doubt that this was a reference to Schapelle's case. It was, said Ford, obvious that Schapelle was a victim of domestic drug trafficking run by petty criminals and cowards.

He was asked for the name of the person who had actually placed the marijuana in Schapelle's luggage, but he shook his head and said he was '100 per cent certain if I mention this person's name connected to this case I will be killed. Very likely Ms Corby as well, just to prove a point.' Why, the judges wanted to know, if he had agreed to speak in her defence, was he unwilling to name the true culprit. Ford said he had been threatened in prison and so had his daughter.

'All I can say to the court is there is no way on God's earth Ms Corby is a drug trafficker. I know better than that. I think the court can see that as well. My belief in that is so strong I will put my personal safety at risk and I am not asking anything in return. I just want to see justice done.'

His evidence appeared to have little influence with the judges and it was not long before he was heading back, under escort, to the cell in Australia he had left behind.

As if the case was not controversial enough, 'Mad Ron' Bakir alleged on a Sydney radio station that the prosecution had looked for a bribe in return for not asking for the death penalty in Schapelle's case. 'It's an absolute disgrace,' Bakir claimed, alleging that the defence had been approached by a person acting on behalf of the prosecutor. The impact in Bali was immediate, an outraged prosecution and government officials demanding an apology for a smear campaign fortified by lies.

So, two witnesses in Schapelle's defence had fallen by the wayside. Apart from the row surrounding Bakir's alleged radio comments, the prosecution, referring to Ford's evidence, said the only reason he had come to Bali from his Australian jail was to taste freedom. 'Discount everything he said,' the judges were urged. What followed were words that sent shock waves through the court, around the island and around Australia. Schapelle Corby, said prosecutor Wiswantanu, was deserving of a life sentence. She had refused to admit her guilt and there was no plausible evidence for how the drugs had got into her bag. The prosecutor's words hung in the air for a second.

She deserved life.

Then chaos broke out. Schapelle, wearing a light blue striped shirt gasped as her lawyer told her what had been said. There were screams, cries of 'No!' and even lawyer Lily Lubis broke down in tears. 'It's not the death penalty,' Ms Lubis told her after composing herself. 'And we are not finished yet. You haven't been convicted. It's only a request.'

Her defence put up every logical, and factual, argument in their arsenal. If Schapelle was intent on taking drugs into Bali, why didn't she take the simple precaution of putting a lock on the boogie board case? And why put the plastic bag containing the drugs on top of the board, where they would be immediately seen by anyone taking a look inside? Importantly, too, was the question why anyone would risk a death or life sentence smuggling marijuana from Australia to Bali, to be sold for much less than the cannabis would get in Australia.

Schapelle now needed to make a heart-felt plea to the judges. Jail for life would effectively mean that her life was on the line. Observers in the courtroom had agreed that the stress Schapelle had shown throughout the case suggested she would not survive year after year in Kerobokan.

She had to explain to the judges why she hadn't admitted the crime she had been accused of – importing a commercial quantity of marijuana. 'I cannot admit to a crime I did not commit,' she said, standing before the judicial bench. 'And to the judges, my life at the moment is in your hands but I would prefer it was in your hearts. I say again that I have no knowledge of how the marijuana came to be in my bag.' She had never claimed ownership of the bag containing the marijuana, the bag had not been fingerprinted, and there was a problem with baggage handling at airports, she reminded them.

'I'm an innocent victim of a tactless drug smuggling network. I believe the seven months which I've already spent in prison is a severe enough punishment for not putting locks on my bags. My heart and my family are painfully burdened by all these accusations and rumours about me and I don't know how long I can survive here. And I swear, as God is my witness, that I did not know that the marijuana was in my bag. Please look to your God for guidance in your judgement of me for God only speaks of justice and Your Honour I ask for you to show compassion, to find me innocent, to send me home.'

Her mother Rose and sister Mercedes sat as close as possible to Schapelle as they all waited nervously on 27 May 2005 for the judges to announce their verdict. Judge Linton Sirait's words were what they did not want to hear. Schapelle Corby, said Judge Linton Sirait, had been found guilty of importing a narcotic into Bali and had 'convincingly carried out a crime'.

She was sentenced to 20 years in Kerobokan.

Schapelle slapped her forehead and sobbed as her mother shouted towards the judge, 'Liar! Liar!' And her eyes fixed on Schapelle as she said, 'Honey, we're going to take you home.'

'Mum, stop, it's okay,' said Schapelle as her mother continued to shout at the judges, who simply rose and made their way from the courtroom. Police surrounded Rose but Schapelle managed to get through to her mother to hug her. Mercedes stood by shaking her head. 'She's innocent. This is not fair.'

Outside the court, lawyer Lily Lubis said she did not think Schapelle would be able to survive 20 long years in a Balinese prison. 'I believe my client, our client, is innocent. She's not deserving of this. It's going to be hard, very hard. I don't think she can survive.'

While Schapelle's family and supporters insisted the punishment was far too harsh for a crime she insisted she had not committed, the prosecution declared that the judges were in error – they should have imposed a life sentence. Both sides, prosecution and defence, announced they were going to appeal the verdict.

Prime Minister Howard showed compassion and urged people in Australia who believed Schapelle was innocent to accept the verdict. Other countries, he said, would resent Australia telling them how to operate their system of justice. He said he asked people to 'accept and understand that when Australians go abroad they are subject to the justice system of the countries they visit.'

And so, a new stage in the life of the former beauty therapist began. She decorated her cell with photos, brightly-coloured bedding, a couple of small cabinets, books. She was a young woman in her prime, yet these were to be her surroundings for many years to come.

But faint hope existed in appeals and pleas for clemency. Two months after the sentencing the High Court ruled in July 2005 that the case should be reopened by the district court, which would allow the defence team to call new witnesses who would be able to prove that Schapelle did not place the marijuana in the boogie board case. A man said to be the owner of the drugs was named as a key witness, but he told officials he knew nothing about the cannabis.

Schapelle received something of a breakthrough in October that year when the High Court reduced the sentence to 15 years, resulting in the defence and prosecution appealing yet again. The new appeal by the defence to the Indonesian Supreme Court proved to be a risk that turned bad – the court overturned the previous 5-year reduction and reinstated the original term of 20 years. The objects that were the focus of so much discussion – the boogie board bag and the marijuana – were ordered to be destroyed. It appeared to be the end of the legal line for the young woman who now sat miserably in her cell.

CHAPTER FOURTEEN

GOODBYE TO THE 'LAST PARADISE' AS THE BOMBS EXPLODE

Until the first Europeans officially stepped ashore in 1597 Bali was a typical far-flung island, its people, living in their grass huts, ruled over by a king who travelled in a shaded chariot drawn by two white buffaloes.

It was Dutch explorer Cornelis de Houtman who made early sketches of life there, including an illustration of the rite of self-sacrifice. But he wasn't the first to touch land. It's thought that Marco Polo was among the pioneers, although the first confirmed contact was in 1512 when Portuguese explorers António de Abreu and Francisco Serrão landed on the north coast. Subsequently, maps drawn by Portuguese and Spanish expeditions referred to the island as Bally, Bale and Boly.

Word spread that the women were beautiful, the reports enhanced by the tale of the survivors of a Portuguese ship which foundered on a reef, who were cared for by the Dalem, King of Gelgel, who provided them with homes and 'wives'.

In 1597, when Cornelis de Houtman arrived, he was stunned by the beautiful long beach stretching out from what is today Kuta. He wasn't going to leave this fantastic place to other foreigners and christened the island Young Holland. Sadly, the growing European influence in a small peaceful land gave rise to exploitation of the locals. Female and male slaves were captured, the women being desirable for their beauty and creativity while the men were popular for their courage and manual skills.

As the decades rolled by, Bali fell under the administration of not only the Dutch but partially by the French, while also being targeted by the British. But the Dutch later resumed authority, telling the royal family that they would stamp out opium smuggling, slavery and the plundering of ships which came to grief in the unpredictable seas around the island. There were numerous clashes, however, between the Balinese kingdoms, giving the Dutch the chance to muscle in and increase control.

Fighting between the Dutch and forces loyal to the kingdoms resulted in hundreds of deaths – in the elimination of the royal house in the Badung regency some 1000 warriors were killed. Massacres of the locals occurred in other parts of the island in clashes with the Dutch, one 1906 photo showing dozens of corpses at Denpasar. The mounting death toll in the southern part of the island between 1906 and 1908 brought international criticism of the Dutch, who agreed to bring their brutal dominance to an end and instead turn Bali into a treasure trove of classic culture.

In order to show the world that peace had finally come, barriers were lowered and the island was opened up to tourism, the first groups being from a regular steamship, which travelled between the neighbouring island of Java and Bali in 1924. The excited travellers would disembark on a Friday morning, travel around the island by car over bone-rattling roads, and sleep in rest houses before departing on the Sunday. The first hotel, not surprisingly named the Bali Hotel, was opened in Denpasar in 1928. Only 300 or 400 tourists visited the island each year in the 1920s but that grew to several thousand in the 1930s – it was really just the start of the destruction of those same cultural values that it had been hoped could be preserved.

In between the old wars and the modern tourist invasion, however, Bali found peace. It was a long way from anywhere European so only the most dedicated of travellers were game enough to head there. Among those who did arrive, in 1922, was German photographer Gregor Krause whose four thousand images revealed to the world life in the villages where women bathed naked and unashamed.

Others who did sail to the island in the 1930s were anthropologists Gregory Bateson and Margaret Mead; artists Walter Spies and Miguel Covarrubias; and musical academic Colin McPhee. Covarrubias was so taken with the island that he wrote that it consisted of 'brown girls with beautiful breasts, palm trees, rolling waves and all the romantic notions that go to make a South Sea Island paradise.'

In contrast, however, Covarrubias had the foresight to note that Bali was in danger of losing its cultural charm. Tourism was growing so rapidly by 1931 that he found the rush of visitors was 'in full swing'. In fact, when he first stepped ashore he noted that 'the beautiful Balinese of steamship pamphlets are not to be seen anywhere. The people on the streets are ugly and unkempt, and instead of the much-publicised beauties there are only uninteresting women in not very clean blouses.'

Yet, by the late 1930s the island's reputation as a place of cultural beauty was largely restored through the propagation of German artist and musician Walter Spies. Visiting Bali for the first time in 1925, after working as the Sultan's director of music in the palace at Yogyakarta, he was inspired to set up a studio in Ubud, from where he spread the word about the wonder of Balinese music, dance and art.

Ironically, his word and his work spread far and wide following his death at sea after he was evacuated from Indonesia during Japanese military rule in 1942. But while he was in Ubud, creative personalities from far and wide had come to visit him, including American dance scholar Claire Holt, British dance scholar Beryl de Zoete, US film producer Andre Roosevelt and German author Vicki Baum. Was what he told the world the reality of life in Bali? Or was the mysticism he portrayed a fantasy of mind? Whatever it was, there is little doubt that one of his paintings, depicting a stick-like peasant walking through a misty 'Garden of Eden' ahead of a buffalo became a tourist magnet.

Through Spies and others who wrote eagerly about the island, Bali earned a reputation as being 'the last paradise', a land of solitude, an enchanted place where the people were at peace with nature and themselves. Charlie Chaplin, following his visit there in 1932, wrote in his autobiography how his elder brother Sidney recommended visiting the island because it was untouched by civilisation and there were 'beautiful women with their exposed bosoms. These aroused my interest.'

Bali clearly had sex appeal and this was emphasised in a number of films that were made about the island, leading to suggestions that it was far from being suppressed and even homosexuality was not hidden like it was in the western world. It was land of contrasts, as even Margaret Mead had noted when she described Bali in a letter as being 'the most extraordinary combination of a relatively untouched native life going along smoothly and quietly in its old way with a kind of extraneous, external civilisation superimposed like an extra nervous system put on the outside of a body.'

The mystical experiences of Westerners who had visited Bali 30 and 40 years earlier gave birth to a 'modern' era of 1950s and '60s rock stars, hippies, dreamers looking for inner peace; or just somewhere to hang out, smoke dope and enjoy a carefree Bohemian lifestyle. The beatniks wore beads, paisley-patterned clothing, ate vegetarian food, sat in the lotus position and enjoyed sex, sex and sex. Outside the simple huts and rooms where the free spirits paid next to nothing in rent, the numbers of motorcycles and cars began to grow each year. Tourists who did not share the laid-back existence of the hippie set strolled into small shops and ran their hands through the racks of batik cloths and fingered the hand-crafted jewellery.

Amid the worsening noise and the petrol fumes, the Western invasion was truly on its way and this time there was no going back. Bali was about to lose its image of tranquil beauty.

• • •

Not in my wildest dreams could I have pictured myself here…walking through a dim corridor where I realised for the first time that I could actually smell blood. There were cries, screams, figures lying on the concrete floor, their legs rolling from side to side as they struggled with their pain. Cries for help – English words, French, Indonesian; no translation was necessary. It was the anguish in the voice, not the word, that carried the plea. A nurse ran past, a bandage unwinding in her hands, but she didn't worry about rolling it back – someone needed it right then. No time for niceties. The voices a chorus of fear and uncertainty, individuals wondering if they were going to live or die for there were serious burns, broken bones, hanging limbs. How many lay there in beds, sprawled on the floor, sitting on chairs? Impossible to know amid such chaos.

You don't want to get in anyone's way, but somehow, they see someone like me who hasn't been injured as a hope to cling to. But what could I do? I wrote down a name, asked what they remembered, where they were hurt, whether they had family somewhere, but I felt like I was intruding. Yet some wanted to talk to me. Perhaps it was a distraction from the pain they were in. A photographer, the late Peter Carrette, who was with me kept muttering 'my God, my God', but he had to get on with his job, too. The world would want to know what happened. There were relatives somewhere far away who might see the photos and be thankful that a loved one had survived. Pete aimed his camera. Nobody cared what he was doing.

Perhaps they were in shock; they looked but didn't see. We didn't need to linger further. I tried to stay calm but I could feel anger. Someone, more than one, did this to these people. And whoever did it was still out there.

'Evil,' I said aloud. 'Just evil.'

It was five minutes past 11 pm on 12 October 2002. Paddy's Pub, located on a restaurant strip about half a kilometre from the Kuta beachfront, was crowded. It was the weekend, a Saturday night, and mothers, fathers, daughters, sons, friends, mates, were enjoying the last hours of their vacation, for many were due to fly home the following day in what local tourism officials describe as 'changeover time' for departures and arrivals.

Music filled the air and the drinks flowed and no-one took any notice of Feri, an Indonesian, as he made his way through the noisy crowd. He was afforded hardly a glance as he reached for a small hidden switch. A second later Feri was blown to piece as his backpack exploded. Screaming tourists, many badly injured ran or staggered out into the narrow street – just as the terrorists behind the cruel plot had planned. For that was the moment, 20 seconds after the explosion in Paddy's, they detonated a second, more powerful bomb hidden inside a white Mitsubishi L300 van parked 'harmlessly' outside the Sari Club, directly opposite Paddy's.

The open-air, thatched roof Sari Club was destroyed in a flash and scores were killed immediately. Nearby buildings collapsed. Windows were shattered hundreds of metres away. The blast was so intense that it left a crater one-metre deep where the Sari Club had stood. Wooden rafters and pillars blazed. Bodies lay everywhere. Dazed, smouldering, survivors stumbled over the smoking debris. In such a narrow street, the effect of the second bomb was made far worse. Human flesh and blood stood no chance in the powerful explosion.

First reports reaching the rest of the world suggested that the chaos had been caused by a major gas leak, but within hours it became clear that the devastation and death was a deliberate act of terrorism – a word that was met with disbelief for Bali, despite its history of feuding kingdoms and wars with the Dutch, and in more recent years rowdy antics by tourists, had been considered a peaceful island. The scenes in those first few hours – at the site of the bombings, in hospitals and medical centres – were unimaginable. The dying, the badly injured, the burned were rushed by ambulance, private car, police vehicles, whatever was available, to medical centres, hospitals, anywhere with a doctor, a nurse, even a medical student, where they could receive urgent attention. Hotels opened their doors to the wounded, who sat crying and shaking from shock. Western doctors who were on holiday hurried to the chaotic area, through the smell of burning as debris, buildings and cars smouldered, to help anyone who needed it.

Terrorism had come to America with the attacks on the twin towers a year earlier on September 11, 2001 and now this, one year, one month and one day later. Were the dates significant? And why such a small island as Bali, when the previous year's attack on the US had greater impact politically and in the number of casualties – although even one death from terrorism anywhere meant that other loved ones had been thrown into unexpected grief.

At the main hospital, Sanglah, the preceding hours had passed routinely. A motor scooter rider with a broken leg, a woman with contractions, nothing that the staff could not cope with. And then came the frantic warning for every doctor, surgeon, nurse, to be ready for a major emergency. Hospital staff were called in from their homes, not bothering to change into their uniforms. As carloads of injured were brought in, beds were soon taken and dozens had to be laid out in the corridors crying out for something to ease their pain.

Pleas for medical assistance went out to nearby countries – Australia, Singapore, Malaysia – to send doctors and surgeons, a cry for help that was soon to be met by other countries that flew doctors and nurses across the world to help. But in the immediate aftermath, so many people were crying in agony from burns that for relief they had to be lowered into hotel swimming pools to ease the pain. Badly burned survivors were flown to major hospitals in Australia, but there was little or nothing that could be done for those who were fatally injured or who had been killed outright.

The death toll rose steadily in the days that followed, the final number of fatalities climbing to 202, the most deaths being among Australians, for Bali's proximity to Australia had made it a popular vacation destination. A total of 88 Australians died as a result of the blasts, followed by 38 Indonesians and 28 British. Other victims were from the US, Germany, Sweden, Holland, France, Denmark, Switzerland, New Zealand, Brazil, Canada, Japan, South

Africa, South Korea, Ecuador, Greece, Ireland, Italy, Poland, Portugal, and Taiwan. More than 200 others were injured, some badly. The variety of countries illustrated Bali's popularity as a holiday destination – and why it was targeted by terrorists looking for a 'big hit'.

The terrorism plot was successful in its execution because those behind it knew that Saturday night would bring large crowds to the nightclubs and, pointedly, no-one who set out that night for holiday fun could have imagined their place of entertainment would be blown up and many of them would be killed.

There were heroes, of course. Too many to name, to single out. But those who went back in, facing uncertain danger, to look for anyone too badly injured to help themselves, were heroes. The tourists who ran from their hotels, past road blocks, to render assistance without a care for their safety, were heroes. The Indonesian people, who helped strangers from other countries, were heroes. And every medical person who tended broken and bleeding victims were heroes. What was bad had brought out the good. Everyday people who had acted spontaneously, who stared at the human carnage and who carried on, were heroes. And what they did emphasised just how vile the perpetrators of the horror were.

Tangled electrical lines, leaning power poles, roof tiles, smouldering vehicles and unrecognisable debris littered the street. Where ordinary people had searched in the immediate aftermath of the blasts, specialist officers and police were soon crawling through the wreckage looking for body parts that would eventually help with identification. The question that was being asked, almost as soon as the carnage had been brought, was who?

Who had such wickedness in their hearts that they could massacre so many people? And of course, why? Police set up road blocks in the hours after the twin blasts, but by then those responsible, apart from the suicide bomber, had had time to get clean away.

Suspicion fell on Java-based terrorists inspired by Osama bin Laden. The killers in the sights of investigators were members of Islamist group Jemaah Islamiya, an organisation that had blown up buildings and killed many in other parts of the country and was led by radical cleric Abu Bakar Bashir, who despite his hatred of the West gave outward appearances of being someone's harmless, white-bearded grandfather.

A search was organised to track down known members of Jemaah Islamiya while investigators worldwide applied their skills to put together the sequence of events. However, the reasons for the bombings came, allegedly, from Osama bin Laden himself, in a recorded voice message played on the Arab satellite channel Al Jazeera a week later. It was all America's fault, he said. He blamed the US for its war on terror in Asia and Australia's role in the liberation of East Timor, which had gained its independence from Islamic Indonesia.

'You will be killed, just as you kill, and will be bombed, just as you bomb,' said the voice. 'Expect more that will further distress you.' A former FBI agent, Ali Soufan, later confirmed that Al-Qaeda had financed the attack, described by Indonesia's police chief General Da'i Bachtiar as being 'the worst act of terror in Indonesia's history'.

Indonesian police began urgent inquiries among their contacts, who had assisted them in the past in fingering members of the terrorist army under Abu Bakar Bashir's leadership. Names came up. Police questioned Aris Munandar, also known as Sheik Aris, and from him they obtained the name of Amrozi. Sheik Aris was thought to have acquired some of the explosive material and passed it to Amrozi.

Quiet inquiries resulted in a police 'SWAT' team raiding a house in Java in the dead of night, where Amrozi was sleeping in the rear. According to one report, he laughed and told police how clever they were. They made a thorough search of the premises, seizing Amrozi's phone. They also found bags of chemical ingredients in his workshop, as well as soil samples that showed traces of the primary chemical used in the Sari Club bomb, an incendiary device described as a 'fertiliser bomb'.

The United States-Indonesia Society said in an official report later that police had also found receipts for the purchase of chemicals in Amrozi's home, along with a list of expenses he'd incurred in building the bombs. The fact he kept such a list suggested he had been paid money to buy the ingredients and had to account for everything he had spent. Ominously, police also found copies of speeches by Osama bin Laden and Abu Bakar Bashir, in which the two terrorist leaders implored followers to wage a holy war on the West.

If these finds were not enough to implicate Amrozi, there was more. Lying on the floor were training manuals on how to carry out an ambush.

But the seized phone was the greatest find of all, for in it police found the names of numerous known Islamists whom Amrozi had spoken to in previous days. Under interrogation in a secret holding cell, Amrozi 'squealed'. He confirmed that others involved in the bombing were Ali Imron, Imam Samudra, Mukhlas (also known as Ali Ghufron), Dul Matin, Idris, Abdul Ghani and Umar Paatek.

The planning had been simple, arousing no suspicion. The United States-Indonesia Society went on to report that Amrozi and fellow bombers Idris and Ali Imron had simply walked into a dealership and purchased a new Yamaha motorbike. They had even asked how much they could sell it for if they brought it back in a few days – a comment that suggested they believed they would get clean away after the dual attacks.

On the night of the bombings, police learned, it was Imron who rode the bike to the US Consulate where he planted a small bomb which, when it went off ahead of the massive nightclub bombings, caused little damage. But it was a clue to the reasons behind the attacks – it was all America's fault.

Imron had then passed the motorbike to Idris, while Imron drove two suicide bombers in the Mitsubishi to the nightclubs. Outside the Sari Club, Imron ordered one of the bombers to put on the suicide vest and the other to arm the bomb that was in the rear of the van. The first bomber, Feri, strolled into Paddy's Pub with the backpack to await instructions. Idris then told the second bomber, named as Arnasan, who had only learned to drive in a straight line, to move the minivan a few yards so that it was close to the Sari Club. Idris had then picked up Imron on the motorbike and the two headed back to Denpasar. The deadly stage was set. From Denpasar, Idris dialled a number on a Nokia phone, which detonated the small device at the US Consulate. Then, under their promise of going to a better place, the suicide bombers exploded their devices, the backpack being worn by Feri and the bomb in the van with Arnasan at the wheel.

Days after the attacks, having spoken to a number of injured in hospitals, I stood with a crowd of disbelieving tourists and local people and stared at the teams of police still sifting through the rubble. There were curses among the spectators, many wept, but the overall mood was not unexpected.

They wanted revenge, not that they were related in any way to the dead and injured, but they could feel for all those affected, as well as their families. 'It could have been one of ours,' said a German woman. 'It could have been one of ours,' she repeated.

With the arrest of Amrozi and other key players came the revelation that the alleged mastermind, Imam Samudra, had stayed on quietly in Bali for a number of days, watching police at the crime scene and ready to alert his terrorist colleagues about any leaked developments, although he is understood to have learned that police had identified Amrozi as being one of the key players.

Australian Federal Police Commissioner Mick Keelty, who had earlier confirmed that the blast at the Sari Club had been caused by a fertiliser bomb of potassium chlorate, aluminium powder – and not, as first suspected a C4 plastic explosive – revealed after five weeks of investigations that good progress had been made.

'We know about the hire car that was used to go to the showroom where the motorbike was purchased from. We know about the chlorate was used...we know about the meetings in various hotels and safe houses in Bali,' he said as the hunt continued for all those among the terror group who were still at large. He said he did not want to raise false hopes about a quick arrest of everybody because 'many of these people travel on false passports, many of these people are experienced at creating false identities.' But, he told the Australian Broadcasting Corporation, 'having their names and knowing the role they played is part of the enterprise, is an important and positive step forward early in the investigation.'

He was asked about Imam Samudra remaining in Bali to keep an eye on how the investigations were proceeding. 'That's not unusual,' he said. 'I mean, these persons are like any criminals. They look to see, look to observe at the response by the authorities to the terrorist act.'

The arrest of Amrozi had opened up a large area of investigation, particularly, said Commissioner Keelty, in identifying the other suspects and their roles. 'But the important thing about Amrozi is that quite a time before his arrest, we had developed a theory about the crime scene ourselves from the crater at the Sari Club and from the intelligence we received from the motorbike.'

Yet Mr Keelty also conceded that despite success in rounding up suspects and those who could easily be seen to be killers based on the discovered evidence, there was a negative side. 'When a terrorist act occurs,' he said, 'in fact, we've failed in one sense to prevent it from occurring.'

At the end of April 2003, after months of interrogation, Amrozi, nicknamed the Smiling Assassin because he grinned whenever a camera was turned on him as he was moved from cell to cell – was finally charged with his involvement in the bombings. Others were to follow, including Imam Samudra, Amrozi's brother Ali Imron and Ali Ghufron.

Amrozi's lawyers, aware that he would almost certainly be sentenced to death if convicted, told the court in Denpasar that he was not one of the masterminds and he had already been wrongly found guilty in a trial by media. However innocent his lawyers had tried to show he was, the tears of the first witness, a heroic traffic warden called Haji Agus Priyanto, brought anger among those witnessing his testimony. Mr Priyanto openly wept as he recalled spending 11 hours pulling bodies from the debris and how people who had not been killed immediately had then died in his arms.

With Amrozi and his younger brother Ali Imron appearing together, Imron said it was Amrozi who had attended a meeting at which Imam Samudra, the alleged mastermind, had discussed potential targets on Bali. Imron said it was decided to hit the nightclubs because they wanted to kill Americans and citizens of other countries who were allies of the US.

'I'm not responsible,' Imam Samudra angrily protested. 'Amrozi was behind this.'

And as the trial of the three men proceeded through 2003 Amrozi admitted that he was involved in other deadly bombings in Indonesia. His hatred for Westerners, he said, had started when he worked in Malaysia where he heard from Australian co-workers about the decadent behaviour of white people visiting Bali.

'I'm not the mastermind of the bombings,' he said, echoing Imam Samudra's claims of innocence, but he admitted he had purchased the explosives and had transported them. Incredibly, using words that signalled his death warrant, he added, 'When I heard on the radio there were many foreign victims, I was very proud.'

It was time to hear from victims themselves. In June 2003 three survivors came to the court to show the judges their injuries. Peter Hughes and Jason McCartney rolled down 'burns stockings' to reveal their scars. Mr McCartney, a former Australian Rules footballer told how he still lived in fear because of 'ugly visions'. A third Australian, Stuart Anstee, told how he could have died when his jugular vein was cut in the blast – and he showed the court the deep scar on his neck.

The prosecution's case against Amrozi, who smiled frequently during his trial, ended on June 30 when the judges were asked to impose the death penalty. Western witnesses in the court were left in no doubt that his days were numbered. As Amrozi was being led from the court, Spike Stewart, a father still grieving for his son Anthony who had been killed in the explosions, jumped to his feet and shouted in Indonesian 'Amrozi, you're dead! Bastard.'

It was time for Amrozi to launch his defence and through his lawyers, on 14 July he claimed, bizarrely, that the main blast might have been caused by the US or Israel exploding a mini nuclear device. The attack, though, he told the court, had had some positive effects because it restored religious and moral standards on the island and stopped the Balinese people from becoming slaves of foreigners.

By the time Amrozi's defence was over, the court had heard evidence against him from 60 witnesses. No-one was surprised on 7 August when Chief Judge I Made Karna read out the court's verdict: Amrozi was guilty and was sentenced to death by firing squad. The guilty terrorist turned to his lawyers, grinned, and gave them the thumbs up.

If this was an attempt to show that he was actually insane and should not have been charged in the first place, no-one was buying it. Clapping and cheering broke out in the public gallery at the verdict. The five judges said in a long summary that the death penalty was justified and would serve to educate others to prevent a repetition of the crime.

'The death sentence should be used for a crime against humanity or an extraordinary crime,' they agreed. They had even quoted extensively from the Koran, rejecting the use of violence in the name of Islam, pointing out that Amrozi and his co-defendants had misused the term jihad, meaning a holy struggle, to justify their actions. 'Islam never teaches violence, murder or any other crime,' said another of the judges, Lilik Mulyadi.

It was time for the verdicts on two other key players for whom the prosecution had asked for death sentences: Mukhlas (Ali Ghufron) and Imam Samudra. The prosecution had described Imam Samudra as the field commander for the bombings and, a brutal fanatic, he deserved to die. He had picked Bali as the target and had raised finances and recruited a bombing team.

In his defence, Samudra said that the US and its allies were a force of terrorists, colonists, and arrogant. The Americans, he said, had killed thousands of people during its war in Iraq. And while not admitting to any of the charges that carried the death penalty, he insisted the bombings were justified.

Finally, it was the turn of Mukhlas to say his piece, calling then-US President George W Bush a terrorist and pointing out the bombings were to avenge the suffering of Muslims at the hands of America and Israel.

Like Amrozi, Imam Samudra and Mukhlas were sentenced to death. All subsequent appeals failed. They were to go before the firing squad.

Under the tightest security, the three convicted men were flown to the 'death island' of Nusakambangan off the coast of central Java. Amrozi was moved there earlier than anticipated after hundreds of protesters, tired of waiting for him to be executed, stormed Kerobokan prison in October 2005, on the third anniversary, shouting 'Kill Amrozi, Kill Amrozi.' There was to be a long wait, during which he remarried his first wife Rahma, in a ceremony conducted in his absence in his home village, while he also remained married to his current wife.

Along with Imam Samudra and his brother, Mukhlas, Amrozi launched a constitutional challenge against the use of firing squads. He would rather be beheaded, he told his lawyers. In any case, he said that revenge would be taken for his death. His move to Nusakambangan was followed by the arrival there of Mukhlas and Imam Samudra. All options by the three terrorists for escaping execution had failed.

In late October 2008 a firing squad held target practice in preparation for the executions. A team of crack police sharpshooters who were among a squad who travelled from their base in Semarang, Central Java, practised their skills, which would entail striking the convicted men in the heart.

All three were doomed to die alone, but at the same prearranged time, tied to posts in a disused prison on the island. Black crosses would be pinned to their chests, over their hearts, and those crosses would have reflective tags on them, which would make the target, illuminated by spotlights, easier to hit.

The firing squads, it was revealed, were made up of single men with no children to avoid possible psychological problems among those who are uneasy about taking another human life – even though none of the men would know who had actually fired the deadly shots. The reason was that several of the SSI rifles, which would fire 5.5 mm bullets, would be loaded with blanks, but should any of the condemned men still be alive after the volley of shots, the commander of each team would complete a coup de grâce to the head with a revolver.

Despite his arrogance, his show of bravado and indifference to his victims during his trial, in the minutes leading up to his execution, Amrozi showed that he was a coward after all. One source told Sydney's *Daily Telegraph* that Amrozi was the least brave of the trio and that as his end neared he was shaking, he looked pale and was terrified of the fate that awaited him.

The prisoners were driven to the place of execution, Nirbaya, some two miles south of the jail. The short journey took longer than expected because a torrential downpour earlier in the day had made the narrow track slippery and the vehicles had problems negotiating it.

When the condemned men were eventually tied to posts, with Amrozi in the middle, Mukhlas to his right and Samudra to his left, three Muslim preachers approached and read verses from the Koran. Bali prosecutor, Ida Bagus Wiswantanu, then read out the execution order in which the men's crimes and their sentences were detailed. Under a moonless sky, black hoods were put over their heads and at 12.15 am on the start of that day of 9 November 2008, the cracking sound of rifles rang out. But not before Mukhlas defiantly called out 'Allah Akbar! Allah Akbar!'

Five minutes later they were pronounced dead. Their bodies were later washed in the Muslim tradition by a brother of Amrozi and Mukhlas and the Muslim clerics. Their bodies were then flown in police helicopter to their villages.

Even though other members of the scheming group of bombers remained at large, the executions of the key players brought some relief to the families and friends who had lost loved ones.

Brian Deegan, an Adelaide magistrate who lost his son Josh in the bombings told the ABC that while he opposed the death penalty he had gained some relief from the executions.

'It's not going to heal the unhealable wound – it's only going to ulcerate it,' he said. 'What it will do is close a chapter in my life.'

And Geoffrey Thwaites, whose son Robert died in the bombings, said the executions would not stop terrorism.

'By executing these three people, the problem hasn't gone away…I think we still have a long way to go,' he said. 'This is only a very small step in the process.'

That the executions were not the end of terrorism was a topic that was debated worldwide, particularly as some representatives of the Islamic world made further threats to Western embassies in Jakarta. Sensitive targets such as hotels and nightclubs were put under protection by patrolling police. Tensions were high in the villages where the men had lived and it took an Islamic leader, Umar Shihab, to put out the message that the attackers 'did not die as martyrs. Those who kill other people cannot die as martyrs unless it is in war for the sake of religion. But we are not at war, so we cannot kill.'

It took years after the bombings for tourists to find the courage to come back to the island – and nervousness returned following the executions. But in time Bali became the fun place that offered something enjoyable for anyone and everyone.

However, there was an anxious end to 2016 when it was revealed in December that terrorists had planned a new bomb attack in Bali, to be carried out over the Christmas-New Year period.

The Australian newspaper revealed that intelligence experts in Indonesia confirmed that a Bali attack had been plotted to co-ordinate strikes in tourist areas, but the wicked scheme was foiled when police killed members of a terrorist group in a raid on a house in Greater Jakarta.

In the premises, where three terrorists were shot dead, police found a bomb, which they defused.

Counter-terror expert Taufik Andrie, based in Jakarta, told the paper that police were still pursuing other members of the group in relation to the planned attacks in Bali.

'The Bali plan is not as big as the first and second Bali bombings, but it's dangerous. They are using high explosives,' he said in reference to the plot against the popular regions of Kuta, Legian, Seminyak and Ubud.

But with the death of the terrorists in Jakarta, the danger planned for Bali passed. And in March 2107, TripAdvisor calmed any fears by describing Bali as the greatest destination on earth, an island that embodies exoticism, dripping in lush vegetation and soaked with spirituality. Sarah Matthews, head of TripAdvisor Destination Marketing for the Asia Pacific region, said the island 'encompassed everything, with its natural attractions, cultural richness and gastronomic adventures.'

Her words were a far cry from the screams of terror that had echoed in a narrow street in Kuta 15 years earlier.

CHAPTER FIFTEEN

'007' TO THE RESCUE

It's a long way from the hallowed halls of Westminster, the seat of the British Government, to the hillside rice paddies of Bali, but they came strangely together thanks to the involvement of a former Indian beauty queen. A bizarre connection, but then the most recent years of Pamela Bordes, a former Miss India, had been beyond imagination.

Pamela had made her way from Delhi to London, where she found employment as a respected researcher in the House of Commons. She was said to be fairly competent and there appears little doubt that her beauty added an exotic splash to her austere surroundings.

What her parliamentary employers were not aware of was that Pamela, then aged 27, had been splashing her beauty about in other places after work – earning 'overtime' as a high-class call girl. It would be a scandal, indeed, if it were to be discovered that there was a prostitute – a word she would always distance herself from, preferring instead to be an 'escort' – in the House of Commons.

For no-one could forget the time in the early 1960s when it was sensationally revealed that the Secretary of State for War, John Profumo, was having an affair with Christine Keeler, the mistress of an alleged Russian spy. There were concerns that Britain's security had been compromised, with suspicions that during sex with the Russian she had deliberately, or innocently, passed secrets to a Communist agent.

Fast forward to 1989 and Pamela Bordes, through her work at the House of Commons, had become a very close friend of Colin Moynihan, then the Minister for Sport in Margaret Thatcher's government. But he wasn't the only one who found Pamela more than fascinating – she could add to her very long list of contacts *Sunday Times* editor Andrew Neil and also the editor of *The Observer*, Donald Trelford. Yes, indeed, Pamela certainly had friends in high places.

Then came the bombshell. Word was out. There was a hooker in the

Commons with access not only to the everyday business of the House but possibly classified information. The newspapers went crazy. The story of Pamela was the biggest headline grabber for years. But even as the front pages were rolling off the presses, Pamela was heading out of town – fast. Despite a massive hunt by journalists, she was nowhere to be seen. Newspapers spared no expenses in searching for her, dispatching reporters to the cities of Europe, the nightspots of New York…even to the nightclubs of Delhi. But Pamela had vanished. She was out there in the world somewhere, but she had skilfully dodged the most relentless journalists.

Move on a week to the Lotus Cafe in Ubud, where Mick Jagger and Jerry Hall had once dined when they were in the village for their wedding that never really was. As the search for Pamela continued around the globe, sitting, purely by chance at one of the tables in the cafe, was an employee of *The Sun* newspaper's advertising department, who was on holiday with his wife. The place was crowded, the food was good and all was quiet and relaxed in Ubud. Gazing around at the other diners, *The Sun* man's eyes were suddenly held by the olive-skinned woman sitting nearby. A glance was all he needed to realise that he was in the presence of the most hunted woman in the UK. Pamela Bordes had made Bali her hideaway destination.

She was sitting with another woman and, while tempted to walk straight over to her and try to elicit some comments, the advertising employee held back. What was needed was a picture. According to the story he later told, he asked his wife to quietly, but quickly, go back to their nearby hotel and get a camera. He judged there was time, because Pamela was still only part-way through her meal. It was, *The Sun* man realised, also important to find out where Pamela was staying.

Eventually, when Pamela and her friend got up to step out into the night, the advertising man was ready. He saw her friend start up a motor scooter, with Pamela climbing into the pillion seat, and no photo had yet been taken. The motor scooter headed back through the main part of the village with *The Sun* man following in a car. He needed that photo; the scooter was heading towards a country area and the opportunity for a snap was slipping away. Moments later a flash went off, the scooter wobbled, and Pamela and her friend came off.

'I'm dying, I'm dying!' she cried as a crowd began to gather. As it turned out, Pamela had been left with cut lips, another gash under her left eye, grazing and a broken front tooth. She returned with her friend, named as Rachael, to a villa where she had been staying, its verandah overlooking a deep valley. A doctor was called and while he was able to treat her wounds, he told her that further medical treatment was required. But by now Pamela was being told by friends in the UK that a photo of her in Bali was being run in *The Sun* – and there was no doubt that Fleet Street journalists would already be on their way. She had to get out of the villa and find another hideout while she looked at ways of getting off the island without becoming the centre of the world's attention. With a long list of male celebrities in her 'little black book' Pamela had some story to tell, which made her Number One Target.

I was among a dozen journalists who descended on Ubud, but by then the 'bird had flown'. At the villa where she had been staying, her friend said she had left and she didn't know where she was. Inquiries were made throughout the village, and then word leaked out that she was still there and had found refuge in an isolated farmhouse. It could not be immediately pinpointed, resulting in journalists wading through acres of rice fields, water up to their thighs in the hope that Pamela would appear somewhere. Finally, local people pointed to a thatched roof house right in the middle of yet another rice paddy some 3 kilometres from the centre of Ubud. It was on higher ground, like a building on a small island. I was among the first of the 'visitors' to reach the thick wooden door and knock, then bang, then call out. But there was no response from the elusive former beauty queen. Was she in there, quietly waiting behind the shuttered windows for everyone to go away?

The scenes were unlike anything the Balinese people, accustomed to a daily routine of toiling in the fields, had seen before, with lines of journalists' rental cars parked along a nearby road, long lenses trained on the farmhouse for any sign of movement. Shifts were organised to watch the house day and night, although night time did make it difficult to see if anyone was escaping. But with a thick, seemingly impenetrable forest at the rear of the house the guess was that any getaway would be through the front or to the sides, and those areas were well covered by lenses.

What no-one had foreseen was the arrival in Bali, straight from London and then up to Ubud, of a handsome solicitor who turned out to be something of a James Bond character. In fact, he could so easily have been sent on his mission to Bali by M, such was his derring-do. As it was, he had been dispatched to far-away Indonesia by friends of Pamela to take care of her affairs – not her sexual liaisons but her dealings with the newspapers, because it was being suggested that if she couldn't beat them she should, perhaps, think about joining them and selling her story for a fortune.

The first thing that 'Bond' needed to do was to get Pamela out of the farmhouse – for that was where it had now been confirmed she was hiding – without her being seen, a task that seemed impossible. But from what I later ascertained, the solicitor managed to get into the thick forest at the rear of the house late at night, push his way through the branches and stealthily wade through the water that surrounded the house. He then climbed up the rear wall and onto the roof, before lowering himself through a hole in the thatch, then leading Pamela out through the rear, through the forest and into the safety of a hotel room – or so the story went.

There was, however, evidence that 'Bond' had been up to some kind of daredevil stunt, for when he summoned everyone to a brief press conference in the Bali Beach Hotel later, his once-immaculate grey suit and black shoes were spattered with mud. And when he pulled at the sharp crease in his trousers, it was revealed he was wearing no socks. He explained he was now Miss Bordes's legal representative and would be reading a statement on her behalf. After that, he said, his role with her for the time being would be over. But it was clear from what he said that Pamela was ready to sell her story.

'Bond' unfolded three crumpled sheets of paper on which the statement had been handwritten. The press coverage to date, he said had suggested that Miss Bordes's activities had had ramifications for national security. 'When the true facts are made known, as Miss Bordes intends, that inference will be shown to be wholly without foundation,' he said. In order to allow her to return to a normal life, she would allow only one news organisation to publish what she had to say. Yes, she was looking for money, which would be a matter for lawyers in London, but she also planned to make a substantial donation to charity.

It soon became clear that a deal had been struck with the *Daily Express* newspaper and a senior executive was already on his way out to Bali to seal the arrangements. She would then be secretly moved to another country where she could receive medical treatment for her facial injuries and where she could tell her story in peaceful surroundings. There was, of course, nowhere more peaceful than the villa she had originally stayed at in Ubud – but not with dozens of reporters and photographers hanging around outside. Teams hung around Ubud, others watched the airport, but there was no sign of Pamela or 'Bond'.

But sometimes sheer good luck occurs, just as it had for the advertising man from *The Sun* who had flown to Bali for a relaxing holiday, only to find he had a 'scoop' on his hands. In another fortunate episode – for the press that is, not so much for Pamela – a photographer 'overheard' a conversation through the doorway of that same hotel where the press conference had been held, and he learned that Pamela was flying out of Bali early in the morning on a flight to Hong Kong for medical treatment.

In the mad hours and days that followed, Pamela was besieged by journalists and photographers as her plane took off from Bali. The *Daily Express* deal passed to the *Daily Mail* and her extraordinary story poured out. And if she had not gone to Bali in the first place, it's possible her amazing life as a high-class call girl might never have been told. As it turned out, she found a new home years later in Goa.

She didn't disappoint with the details when she eventually revealed her story. Relaying her life and times to me in her first interview she was able to name names of those she had slept with – big names who included royalty and Libya's Colonel Gadaffi. When asked if that was everyone, she shook her head and laughed. 'Oh no,' she told me. 'There are more.'

'Who?' I asked.

'Have you got an atlas?' she said.

• • •

Pamela was not the only person who wanted to fly to Bali and be far away from the House of Commons as another scandal erupted. Ten years later, in

August 2009, we saw Conservative MP Alan Duncan – later to be appointed a Knight Commander of the Order of St Michael and St George – on a Singapore Airlines flight on its way from London's Heathrow Airport to Denpasar. Behind him he was leaving a row over the use of his government expenses following allegations he had spent them on personal outlays. He had claimed more than £4000 in expenses over a three-year period for fixing up his garden, plus another £600 to maintain his ride-on lawnmower.

Just as in the days when what seemed like half of Fleet Street had been hunting for Pamela, another group of journalists from London were eager to find Mr Duncan wallowing in the Bali sunshine as the row continued in the House of Commons.

What had given his flight to Bali a 'bad look' was his reported comment that British MPs were living on rations and were being treated like 's**t.' On the seat beside him as the jet carried him towards his exotic destination was his partner, James Dunseath, a fact that further enraged opposition MPs as they envisaged the two men having fun in the Far East without an apparent care about the rage in London.

For the journalists who arrived in Bali behind the 52-year-old silver-haired MP there was a problem. His location on the holiday island was unknown and, given the enormous number of hotels, the search for Mr Duncan presented a big challenge. I joined in the hunt for him, phoning numerous resorts, but there was no listing – not that I expected him to be registered under his, or Mr Dunseath's name. But sometimes Lady Luck calls. I came across a local person who knew his movements. Yes, he had flown to Bali. But he didn't stay. He and his partner boarded another jet and hopped across to Lombok, a short 30-minute flight.

There are fewer hotels on Bali's neighbour, so further door-knocking finally tracked down the exclusive villa on the north-west coast of the island – at the end of a potholed road and surrounded by coconut trees – where the two were staying. It was so private, in fact, that black-shirted security guards were not only on duty at the closed front door, but on the beach immediately in front of the premises.

'Who are you? What are you doing here? This is private property.' The protests from the guards came thick and fast when I asked to see Mr Duncan. I was greeted with shaking heads and many fingers pointing me away. A stroll along the beach front, when I hoped to enter the premises legally from that side, was met with the same panicky response from the guards who ordered me to leave the area immediately. Which I did – but not before sighting Mr Duncan stretched out on a sun lounger, his partner beside him. The men were staying in one of two beach pavilions at a cost of around £500 ($850) a night.

The wages of the staff of 18 caring for Mr Duncan's every need were a sharp contrast to his own wealth; while the former oil trader was worth millions, the average wage of a hotel worker, many of whom lived locally, was £2.50 ($4.30). Of course, Mr Duncan had every right to spend his personal money as he wished – but he might also have been wishing that his alleged use of government expenses for personal household expenditure had not come to light and that he had not complained about MPs living on rations.

When his holiday was over, he flew back to Bali, where he was photographed having a drink in a bar prior to his departure. He continued to rise through the ranks of the British Government and in 2016 assumed the office of Minister of State for Europe and the Americas. As for the expenses row, it was reported that he had told then-Prime Minister David Cameron that he would return the 'garden expenses money' to the fees office.

CHAPTER SIXTEEN

DEATH OF A POLICEMAN

Sara met David, they fell in love and they went to Bali for a holiday. If it sounds like the start of a wonderfully romantic vacation, it turned out to be anything but that. For they never came back to Australia. Not that David, an Englishman, could, without applying for a new visa. But Sara fully expected to return to her beachside town of Byron Bay in northern New South Wales in a week's time. Neither dreamed that within a few days they would be in prison, under arrest for an alleged murder. Worse, the victim was a policeman.

Sara Connor, 45, was one of those people whose personality attracted others to her. She ran a pasta business in the town and had made a great success of it, with commercial outlets all around the region. She also worked at the Arts Factory Lodge as a manager. Her two sons meant the world to her, raising them with their father, Anthony Connor – known as Twig – whom she had met, as a single woman called Sara Pistidda, in London while she was on a world trip.

They married in a suburban town hall where, true to the colourful outlook both had on life, guests wore South Pacific floral shirts. On their return to Australia, they purchased a block of land near Yamba in a cornfield at the mouth of the Clarence River. Twig ran a pub while child-loving Sara found work in an orphanage. Next they opened a coffee shop and in between hours Sara held Italian lessons.

The travel bug was still in them and they headed off to Europe, settling in Berlin, where Twig ran a bar. Eventually they returned to Australia in 2010 settling back in Byron Bay. But the marriage to Twig was beginning to crumble. Husband and wife were destined to meet other people, especially as she began to mix with music bands who hung out in Byron Bay or who passed through. In particular she enjoyed the company of a group that played reggae at the Beach Hotel.

Into her life came David Taylor, a 34-year year old dreadlock-wearing

Englishman from Halifax. He came and went from Byron, but finally settled into the town in 2014. With his musical background, he found work as a DJ and announcer on the local community radio station, hence his nickname of DJ Nutzo. By all appearances, with his long locks, beard and loose, colourful clothes, he could have passed for a throwback from Ubud's 1960s hippie period. He had settled comfortably into the lodge where Sara was working and from their frequent chats a close friendship developed. By early in 2016 their friendship turned to romance, but they decided to keep the relationship to themselves, as best they could. She had been single for three years after her marriage had collapsed and she had put all her energy into her pasta business. She wanted Byron Bay to know her simply as a businesswoman, not someone who had found a new partner in David Taylor, the local DJ.

But a problem, which neither of them could have foreseen, was brewing. Taylor, who had travelled the world for years, spending time in New Zealand before settling in Byron Bay, had been married to an Australian woman. Believing she was doing the right thing, she had told the authorities that she and her husband had separated – information that affected his right to remain in the country under his visa category. He was told he would have to leave, then apply to come back again. Aside from New Zealand, the nearest foreign country that had any appeal was Indonesia – and the island of Bali in particular.

Following his last stint as a DJ on BayFM radio, on 22 July 2016, he made plans to fly to Bali. And there was one obvious question he had to ask Sara: 'Will you come and join me for a few days?' She could hardly resist the offer, considering their love for one another.

He arrived in early August, passing the days in cheap hotels and noisy bars as he waited for his true love to turn up. And when her plane touched down shortly after 2 pm on 16 August, he was at the airport to meet her. He'd hunted around for a reasonably priced, clean hotel in Legian, the neighbouring suburb to Kuta, and reached a deal with the management of the Kubu Kauh Beach Inn for a discounted rate of $20 a night. A five-minute stroll from the beach, the inn described itself as giving its guests the 'true Balinese experience', with clean rooms and flat screen TVs, free wi-fi and a basic breakfast thrown in. 'It is ideal for backpackers or the budget traveller in Bali looking for clean, comfortable accommodation; this is right on the beach,' the Balinese family who run it proudly claimed. Amusingly, the family pointed out that 'we have some little dogs and cats that do bark sometimes but are very friendly.'

Connor and Taylor wandered down to the beach in the evening to watch the famous sunset. They strolled along hand in hand before heading to a small restaurant for dinner. It was the perfect start to their holiday, when they discussed their future. Taylor planned to apply for a re-entry permit to Australia while in Indonesia, but if that wasn't successful he would, as a British citizen, possibly have to return to the UK to make the application. But that was later. They had each other for the time being.

After their evening meal they bought a beer each and wandered down to the beach again, sitting on the sand and chatting. They were in a quiet part of the beach where the only illumination was from a full moon. For two people in love, their arms around one another, the setting was idyllic. So idyllic that they decided to wander down to the water's edge. They left their beers and Sara's small black handbag behind and skipped down to the water, where they paddled and once again held one another close. Returning to the place where they had been sitting, Sara searched around then asked, 'Where's my bag? It's not here.'

She began to grow frantic, for inside were her driving licence, credit card and some $300.

They circled around the area in the dim light and it was then that Taylor came face to face with a figure standing near an entranceway onto the beach. 'Someone's stolen a bag,' Taylor said, a question in his statement. The figure, Taylor was to relate later, just said 'ooh', then opened his jacket to reveal a uniform showing that he was a police officer.

Taylor asked the officer, named later as 53-year-old Wayan Sudarsa, to help with the search but in response, said Taylor, the policeman just laughed at him. He became convinced that the policeman knew something about the stolen bag because he was the only person around that part of the beach at that time. It was then that Taylor made a move that was to change not only his own life, but that of Sara, whose only mistake up to then had been to leave her bag on the beach when she ran down to the water.

Taylor's mistake was to step up to the policeman and start patting him down. In turn, Sudarsa grabbed hold of Taylor and threw him to the sand, where the two men wrestled and punched one another. The Englishman was to claim that he was so shocked and scared that he grabbed a pair of binoculars, hanging on a cord around the policeman's neck and hit him in the face with them. Looking for another 'weapon' he grabbed a mobile phone that was lying on the sand and used that to beat at the officer's face. The two men, according to Taylor's account, were now locked in an ugly battle, with Taylor fearing he would die when the officer jammed his right elbow into his throat. Taylor snatched up a large Bintang beer bottle from the sand and smashed it into the back of Sudarsa's head time and again until it shattered.

Until the fight began, Sara Connor had continued looking for her bag, thoughts of her dream romantic holiday being ruined if she had to spend the coming days reporting the loss to the police and contacting Australia to cancel her ATM card. There was also the loss of the $300, which would have gone a long way in Bali. But as she searched, she heard the men brawling and stumbled across the beach to stop the fight. She grabbed hold of Taylor and tried to pull him away, then thrust herself between the two men, desperately trying to separate them. She lost her balance and fell straight down onto the policeman, straddling him, she was to recall. It was then that he bit her on the arm and thigh.

The already desperate situation, with a tourist wrestling with a policeman and beating him about the head with a beer bottle, escalated when Taylor turned the badly wounded officer onto his back and took his wallet and his phone. Connor was horrified at the entire run of events. She told Taylor they had to make a report at the police station and she hurried up to the street and tried to hail a motorbike taxi. The rider refused to take her because she didn't have any money. The couple then made their next mistake; leaving the wounded officer where he lay on the beach, they walked back to the hotel. Taylor told Connor the officer would be okay, he had just passed out. Connor had by now been on the island for just 12 hours and had enjoyed just 5 hours of daylight.

They had showers and Taylor washed his clothes, while Connor set about using a pair of scissors to cut up the policeman's identity cards. The curious reason for doing this, she was to claim later, was to ensure that no-one could use them illegally. Until then she had no idea of the degree of injuries sustained by officer Sudarsa.

The following morning the couple kept to their previous plans and checked out of the Kubu Kauh Beach Inn to search for a hotel in another part of the tourist area. Somewhere that was quieter. They left their bags with reception, arranging to pick them up later once their search for another place was over, and headed for the Jimbaran area. On the way, they threw away a garbage bag containing the policeman's chopped-up ID cards. Then they carried on like the romantic couple they had started out as the previous day before the night-time drama on the beach. They went for a swim at Jimbaran beach and enjoyed lunch beside the sea. Then they checked into a local hotel.

The following day, a Thursday, the couple went to the fish market, strolled about and enjoyed meals by the ocean. Sara was worried about her car registration back in Australia and switched on her phone on the Friday to make arrangements for it to be paid. But as soon as the phone came on, she was astonished at the number of text messages she saw. They were from friends desperate to know how she was and asking her to call them urgently. Her friends had heard news on the radio that a 45-year-old Byron Bay woman was wanted in Bali for the alleged murder of a local policeman.

What she had not known up to that point was that Officer Sudarsa's body had been found on the beach the morning after the fight. Photographs of the two lovers were on police 'Wanted' posters and their pictures were on the TV news. This, Sara was to insist later, was the first time that she and Taylor had learned that the policeman they had struggled with three nights earlier had been found dead with 42 wounds, many apparently caused by a broken beer bottle. His body had, in fact, been found at 3.30 am on 17 August, not long after the fight. Her friends urged her by phone to go immediately to the Australian Consulate. She was stunned. A week earlier she had been happily making pasta in Byron Bay, having fun with Taylor, meeting friends – and now in Bali she was wanted for murder. It had not been difficult for police to suspect who the policeman's assailants might be for Sara's New South Wales drivers licence, one of the items she had searched for, along with her bag, had been found at the scene.

'We should burn all our clothes,' Taylor suggested, referring to the items they had collected from the first hotel. She agreed to do what he said and they found a quiet place to burn the clothing, and Taylor, still in possession of the policeman's mobile phone, smashed it against a wall. Then they made their way to the Australian Consulate where Taylor remained outside because he was a British citizen. Police had already expected the pair to turn up at the Consulate because they really had nowhere to go. The couple were arrested and warned that they could be charged with the murder of police officer Wayan Sudarsa.

At Denpasar police station they were subjected to tough questions, including checks on their wounds to establish if they were fresh. Sara was found to have marks on her hand and leg. Police Chief Purnomo said the couple, who had been separated, gave different versions of events, although both admitted being at the scene of the fight. They were officially named as 'suspects' prior to their possible charging.

To make matters worse for the couple – if they could ever be worse – when the body of officer Sudarsa, who had served in the police force for 30 years, was cremated in a traditional Hindu ceremony, hundreds of people attended, including senior officers in the Balinese police force. Suppressed anger was directed against the pair.

After days of questioning, Taylor admitted he had struggled with the policeman after he had confronted him about Sara's missing handbag. He had used a beer bottle, along with a 'sharp object' he had found in the sand, the policeman's binoculars and a mobile phone to strike him.

Taylor's lawyer Erick Sihombing told reporters that at the end of the fight his client had gone to the street where he had found Connor and he had told her, 'The bag is already gone, so let's go back to the hotel… On Friday, the 19th August, they found blood on their clothes and trousers and hair. That's why they tried to get rid of them by burning their clothes.'

Sara's lawyer, Erwin Siregar, said she had insisted she was not involved in the death of the policeman. 'Sara tried to separate David and the victim, but she could not do it and then because of that the victim bit the right hand of Sara and also the leg on the left side.' She had recalled asking the policeman, 'Where's my bag, where's my bag?'

Friends back in Byron Bay who had expected to see photos of the couple enjoying themselves in the sunshine of Bali were shocked at the images which emerged through the newspapers and on TV. For instead of their beach dress they were seen wearing the bright orange clothes of

Indonesian prisoners, bearing the words on the back: Prisoner of Denpasar Police. Even more humiliating, they were ordered to participate in a re-enactment of that fatal night.

They were escorted back to the beach at night on 31 August and a police officer lay down on the sand, imitating the position of officer Sudarsa. They were told to act out a kiss by the edge of the sea before the next part of the brutal re-enactment got under way. The various 'scenes' were like a movie being shot, particularly as one officer was heard to say as cameras rolled, 'Act seven, David and Sara return from the water's edge, find the bag and the bottle missing.'

On cue, the couple showed how they had searched for Sara's handbag, before Taylor mimed how he had frisked Sudarsa on suspicion he had picked up the bag.

'Act 13, the victim pushed David,' a police voice uttered.

Next, Taylor was ordered to show how he had struck the policeman. He knelt beside the actor clutching the neck of a broken Bintang beer bottle and showed how he had hit Sudarsa as he lay face down in the sand. While this scene was being played out, Connor sat under a tree, biting her nails in anguish. Then Connor was ordered to kneel over the stand-in, just as she said she had done while trying to separate the officer and Taylor. Her lawyer, Erwin Siregar, said it should be clear that she had tried to intervene in the fight to protect the policeman.

'I don't see why my client should be involved in this murder,' said Mr Siregar, insisting that several of the scenes that were acted out were not known to her – a suggestion that Taylor had given police a different version of the events that night. 'The points are, she tried to separate them, she tried to protect the victim. After that happened the biting on her hand and leg took place. Then she left David and the victim to look for her missing bag.'

However, Taylor's lawyer, Mr Haposan Sihombing, suggested that Connor's role in the officer's death was greater than that portrayed. 'Based on my client's statement, they did it together. What's clear was that Sara was there.' This comment tended to support the words of the head of Denpasar Criminal Investigations Reinhard Habonaran Nainggolan who said Connor had admitted during her earlier questioning that she had hit the victim more than once with a mobile phone.

Altogether, a total of 68 scenes were re-enacted, not only on the beach that night, but later at the hotels where the couple had stayed in Kuta and Jimbaran and also in the place at Puri Gading, near Jimbaran, where they had burned their clothes. Close to the burned clothes, police had found the policeman's smashed mobile phone in bushes.

A number of memorable scenes had been played out. But one of the most poignant for the watching police and lawyers had come at the end of the beach re-enactment: Connor and Taylor held one another and kissed briefly before they were taken away separately.

Sara's former husband, Anthony 'Twig' Connor, the father of her two young sons who were still in Byron Bay, had flown to Bali just two days before the re-enactment to give her his support as she waited in a Denpasar cell to learn what charges would be laid against her. It was described as being 'a tearful 15-minute meeting', and he insisted she was not guilty of murder and that she was a 'wonderful person'.

The news neither of them wanted, but had braced themselves to expect, came on 11 October 2016, when prosecutors confirmed the lovers would face three charges: murder, violence causing death, and assault occasioning death. To await their trials, they were taken to Kerobokan prison.

Taylor made it known that he wasn't going to defend the charges, even writing a letter, in Indonesian and English, to the policeman's widow, Ketut Arsini, telling her, 'I really cannot believe that my terrible actions may have contributed to the taking of another life.' Starting his spidery handwritten letter he told her he was sure she would be shocked and angry to be hearing from him but he hoped she could find it in her heart to take a moment to read the letter. He had, he said, been waking up crying for many days, but he could not imagine the pain and suffering that she and her family had to be feeling.

'I will never throughout the rest of my days come to terms with this and it will haunt me until I myself am taken from this life. There is nothing more precious in our lifetime than another human life that we love and care for. I cannot begin to tell you how truly deeply sorry I am for my involvement in this act. I am by no means attempting to explain my actions or ask for your forgiveness. Please just see this as an apology to your whole family from the bottom of my heart.'

The policeman's widow had no intention of forgiving Taylor, even though he said he wasn't asking for it.

She was angry, and she directed her rage towards Connor, claiming that her husband could still be alive if the woman from Byron Bay had tried to find help for him after the incident on the beach. 'If she is such a good person, why did she leave my husband like that?' she asked in an interview with *The Sydney Morning Herald*. 'If she was really trying to help, if she got help, maybe they could have saved him. They just left him. He was found much later. No good person would do that. That's just her excuse.'

As for Taylor's letter to her, she said her first impulse was to rip it to shreds when she saw who it was from. After reading it, she still wanted to tear it up. 'I can't forgive him. We can't forgive him. Whatever they are saying, that it was an accident, they didn't mean it, are all just excuses…the law will take care of them for what they did.'

If it was an accident, she said, why had Taylor hit her husband repeatedly, failed to get help for him, not reported the incident to the police? Why, she wanted to know, had they loosened his belt, taken his wallet and phone, fled to Jimbaran and cut up his identity cards?

Their trials officially began on 9 November, although it was arranged that their cases would be heard separately. They became long, drawn out affairs, with Taylor's case proceeding first. With his dreadlocks now cut off, and dressed in a blue shirt and dark trousers for his court appearance, he admitted hitting the policeman and insisted he had still been breathing when he and Connor had left the beach. Connor had suggested cutting up the officer's ID 'to protect him' because in Australia, 'if someone finds a card they can take it and use it.'

During the fight with officer Sudarsa, he said, he felt in grave danger. 'He was pressing pretty hard on my throat. I couldn't breathe very well. I'd never been in this situation before and I was very scared. I was scared for my life.'

Connor testified at Taylor's trial and he, in turn, was called as a witness in her case. He had admitted beating the policeman and she agreed she had tried to stop the fight. But what did emerge from post-mortem evidence was that Sudarsa had taken two hours to die and according to Dr Dudut Rustyadi he could have been saved had he been taken to hospital.

The verdicts were due to be handed down on Monday, 13 March 2017, despite the trials being held separately. Standing at the bars of a holding cell at the court Sara appeared stressed and said she had not been able to sleep. And she said she was expecting the worst, which at best would be many years in Kerobokan jail. She admitted she had lost all hope of seeing her two sons, aged 9 and 11, growing up in Australia. Prosecutors had already asked that she and Taylor should be convicted of group violence causing death and be sentenced to 8 years in jail, although the maximum is 12 years. Prosecutors had determined not to press for a murder conviction given the evidence that the lovers had not realised the police officer was dying when they left him on the beach.

David Taylor was the first to learn of the judge's decision. He was to be jailed for six years. He said he accepted the verdict and thanked the judges. With the seven months he had spent behind bars he would be a free man after five and a half years. He heard the judges say that he had been polite in court, had never been in jail before and he had apologised to officer Sudarsa's family. His parents, John and Janet Taylor – his father is a church minister – were in court to hear the verdict, after which Mr Taylor said he and his wife were content with the sentence.' But he added that they both believed their son feared for his own life that night and his actions reflected that.

It was Sara Connor's turn to hear what her immediate future held. Chief Judge Made Pasek dismissed her claim that her only role on that fateful night was to try to separate the two fighting men. Instead, said the judge, she had jumped on the policeman's shoulders, effectively pinning him down. 'The defendant's action was not to separate them but to help David Taylor so that the victim could not fight back.'

Connor sat quietly as the sentence was handed down. It could have been much worse than the four years she was given, particularly as the judges said that she had cut up Sudarsa's ID cards not in an effort to protect him from fraud, but out of 'guilt for what she did.'

Listening to her lawyers' advice that if she appealed against the sentence there was a risk it could be increased, she decided to appeal in any case in the hope that if successful she would be home with her sons sooner. In a letter to the appeal court judges she pointed out that she was 'a single mother with two children who need my attention as a parent. The four years was something that was very hard for me and my children…Let me learn from my mistake and be a better person.'

In May came the result of her appeal. Connor's prison time had been increased by a year, so she would be spending five years behind bars. She was not in court to hear the bad news. One of the High Court judges who heard the appeal said the lower District Court had ignored two aggravating factors when it had sentenced her. She had left the victim and had not tried to help him, even though he was still face down – and she had 'damaged Indonesia's tourism image, specifically Bali tourism,' said the judge.

Will Sara Connor and David Taylor get back together once they have served their jail time?

It's a question that perhaps even they were unable to answer as they looked at the years of captivity that lay ahead.

CHAPTER SEVENTEEN

FOREIGNERS AND DRUGS

With her jet-black hair pulled back, her arm tattoo and slender appearance, she might, at first glance, be mistaken for Sara Connor, who had been jailed over the policeman's death. Most outstanding of all, in any photo comparison, was the women's similar attire – the bright orange uniform of a prisoner of Denpasar police.

But the woman who wore the number 32 on her clothing on that day in April 2017 was from a country far from Sara's Australia. Identified only as GNA she was Russian and she stood with hands clasped for an official police photo with three other drug suspects in the Denpasar police station. Her alleged crime was possession of 0.37 grams of crystal meth and she had bought it, she said, from the most unusual of places considering where the seller was located. For GNA, 29, told police that she had purchased the drug from someone inside Kerobokan prison. She wasn't a prisoner, so police considered the sale to be 'unusual'.

'We're investigating who supplied the drug,' said Denpasar Police narcotics division chief Commander I Gede Ganefo. 'She said it was for personal use.' The woman had told police that she had been a user for a year and became completely hooked.

GNA had been living in Bali for eight years, it was revealed, but what she was doing in the prison – perhaps visiting someone who was an inmate and who had access to the flow of narcotics within the mould-stained walls – was still under investigation.

'I need the drug to help me work,' she told police. 'I found I was more focused and got more inspiration when under the influence of meth.' If convicted of possession under the narcotics law, she faced returning to Kerobokan, this time as a prisoner, to serve out a sentence that could be as long as 12 years.

Just one month earlier, a Russian man identified only as AP and an American woman, CL, were arrested after police learned of a plot to smuggle drugs from overseas into Bali through the postal service. The woman had been sent 1.2 grams of meth from the US, while the man was also nabbed for a similar attempt involving 100 grams of ecstasy.

The woman had been difficult to track down, said police, because she had been waiting to receive the package through a post office box, and when it had arrived she held off coming to pick it up for a month. When she finally turned up at the address she was arrested.

The Russian woman identified only as GNA wasn't the first woman from that country to be caught with drugs in Bali in recent years. In 2014, two weeks before Christmas, Aleksandra Magnaeva, 26, tried to pass through Bali customs with 2.1 kilograms of crystal meth in two of her bags. Anyone convicted of trafficking that amount, worth millions of dollars, faced the death penalty. Like for so many others who attempt to smuggle drugs onto the island, the risks are enormous. Customs officials are aware of most of the tricks, and the excuses, which were mostly 'I didn't know those drugs were in my luggage.'

Aleksandra had been living in China with her boyfriend and it was he who had asked her to take the drugs to Bali on a tortuously long and risky route, and finally pass them to someone on the island. She had carried the drugs overland from mainland China to Hong Kong, from where she had caught a flight to Bali. Unless her movements were being watched all the time and officials were tipped off that she was a drug mule, she succeeded in getting the narcotics out of the Chinese mainland, into Hong Kong, through Hong Kong airport and onto the flight to Denpasar.

She might have felt confident that she would get away with it because, according to Bali airport customs chief Budi Harjanto, she claimed she had carried drugs throughout Asia, including to Thailand, 'numerous times'. Harjanto said his officers had detected similarities in the case of Aleksandra and that of a New Zealand man who had been caught trying to smuggle crystal meth into Bali a week earlier. 'We're yet to establish whether the two cases are linked,' said the customs chief.

A dire future lay ahead for the boastful – and brazen – Aleksandra for within a few days of her arrest newly-elected Indonesian President Joko Widodo had made it clear there would be no pardons for drug traffickers already on death row and anyone newly arrested with what would be considered to be commercial quantities of narcotics could face the firing squad if convicted.

Yet still the drugs poured into Bali, bypassing sharp-eyed customs officials before eventually finding their way into nightclubs and villas occupied by hard-partying tourists, locals and expatriates – bule, white foreigners. It was an all-round risk for those involved, whether the drugs were found coming into Bali, when they were picked up, or when they were being used.

Ironically, while the drug laws in Indonesia are among the strictest in South-East Asia, the use of narcotics is extremely high in Bali and the rest of the country. Just why they are in such demand – and easy to get – is often blamed on the lack of resources to watch the entire country, not only its airports but also its seaports. And of course, there are the sheer numbers who pour into Bali daily; it seems inevitable that drugs – heroin, cocaine, meth, marijuana – will get through, ready to be offered in nightclubs or on the streets. It's meth and ecstasy that will be proffered in the clubs and in darkened laneways, while the heavier material will find its way to private addresses where it can be taken in quiet surroundings more conducive to getting high against an exotic background.

Paradoxically, while the risks of 'pushing' are high, dealers in the popular tourist areas, in particular Kuta, Legian and Sanur, are in abundance. They appear to have a knack of approaching the type of tourists who might be ready to buy. Among offerings in plenty are 'magic mushrooms' and cannabis. And there's a powerful explanation for why the dealers show no fear of arrest, for it is frequently whispered that many of them are working with drug police. The dealer gets the purchase money, the police get a feather in their cap for the arrest and the drugs go back on the market.

In October 2016 police presented for public shaming an unexpected figure, David Fox, a British former war correspondent and former bureau chief for Reuters in Jakarta. He'd been a journalistic hero and now he was a suspected drug user. Fox, 54, stood with Australian Giuseppe Serafino, 48, for the 'shame' photo after they were allegedly arrested for possessing a small amount of hashish between them – 17 grams. Each had given police their reasons for using the drug, Fox saying he had started using it after tense times covering stories in dangerous conflict areas which included Somalia. Drugs in those frequently lawless lands were also easily available.

For his part, Serafino said he had used cannabis to increase his appetite and for cancer therapy.

With the men facing anything between 5 and 20 years in jail, there was more to be alleged. Drug Squad officers said that after reading numbers listed on Fox's phone they were also investigating a military officer who was in the country's national security force, the TNI, and a policeman who was with the narcotics division. A sting was set up to buy meth from the two unidentified men. It wasn't long before police announced that they had arrested the military officer and the policeman.

Speaking of Fox and Serafino, Denpasar's deputy chief of police Nyoman Artana said the arrests had followed a tip off. 'We found a report from the community that two foreigners are allegedly using narcotics,' he said. 'We investigated more and on October 8 we arrested an Australian after searching his room and finding 7.32 grams of hashish.' The military officer was handed over to military police while the narcotics squad officer was still being questioned by his colleagues.

The marijuana had allegedly been found at Serafino's residence in Sanur, where he had been living for some five years. On his arrest, he led police to the Briton, who, he alleged, he had bought the drug from. Fox, said police, had been found in possession of about 10 grams of marijuana, some of which was hidden in a boxing glove.

When he later appeared in court, in February 2017, charged with possession of the drug, Fox said he had used it to help him cope with post-traumatic stress disorder following two decades of covering wars. 'Everywhere from Chechnya, Bosnia, Somalia, Afghanistan, Iraq…everywhere in the last 20 years where there's been a war, I've covered it,' he told the judges. He had become addicted to the drug and it had helped him sleep. His addiction had led to the breakdown of his marriage to author Elizabeth Pisani. 'The PTSD and the use of narcotics was all part of the divorce, yes, unfortunately,' he told the court. He insisted he did not deal drugs; the hashish, which he had bought in a Sanur bar from another foreigner, was for his personal use.

When Serafino appeared in court in that same month he apologised for using the drug, saying he did not realise that using cannabis was a big criminal offence. 'I use it to treat back pain,' he said, pointing out he had bought hashish regular from a dealer he would meet in the McDonald's car park in Sanur. He was introduced to the dealer, who was always wearing a motorcycle helmet with his face masked, by his friend David Fox.

In March 2017, Fox was sentenced to seven months imprisonment, after which he thanked the judges for 'the lenient sentence'. Having already served the majority of his sentence he was due for release in a few weeks. The same sentence was imposed on Serafino and in May both men were released from prison and were told to make preparations for their deportation.

'I hope to come back to Bali,' Fox told reporters before his departure. 'I'm very sorry for what happened. It is a good, hard lesson.' Through his lawyer, Serafino expressed the same sentiments.

Pick a year, any year, since the start of the new millennium and it is likely that at least one foreigner will have ended up in Kerobokan, either on remand or as a convicted prisoner, for a drug offence. There are no stereotypes among the arrested – they don't all have long hair and tattoos and look like everyone expects a drug addict or dealer to look. Narcotics officers working undercover at the airport are trained to spot drug mules, those who have something about their appearance or behaviour that doesn't quite fit.

There have been cases of tourists trying to leave the island after a month of surfing, yet they don't have suntans. So why the lie? What have they been up to? Pull them over. Slim women in baggy trousers look oddly out of shape because of the bulges under their clothing. There's nervousness, something in the eyes. They might hesitate at the X-ray machine, waiting momentarily to load their suitcase with a pile of luggage belonging to other travellers in the hope that the drugs in their own baggage will be missed.

It was the 'body language' of Indian traveller Sayed Mohammed Said, 29, that proved his undoing when he arrived at Bali airport on a flight from Bangkok in September 2015. It was, customs officers said, 'suspicious', without specifying what had caught their eye in Said's behaviour as he collected his luggage from the conveyor belt. He loaded his bags into the X-ray machine and what they saw led to them ordering Said to come with them. Inside his backpack officers found a plastic bag, covered in black tape, containing 1.5 kilograms of crystal meth.

With sweat running down his face, Said said the drugs belonged to a

Nepali friend whom he had met in Bangkok and that he was supposed to hand the package over to another person in Bali. He insisted he did not know the bag contained drugs. 'The bag was owned by my friend from Nepal,' he said. 'It's not mine.'

But police believed he was far from innocent, narcotics unit chief Commander Joni Lay announcing later that Said was part of an international drug ring. 'After his arrest, we launched a follow-up investigation, but we haven't yet been able to identify the person [he was intending to pass the drugs to].' In March 2016 Said sat in Denpasar court mopping his brow with a handkerchief as he waited for his sentencing following his conviction. He was told he would go to jail for 14 years. One and a half kilograms of crystal meth was a large amount and he could have received an even longer sentence.

But even the tiniest amount of drugs could land someone in serious trouble, as Sydney fashion model Michelle Leslie, 24, found out in 2005. She had arrived in Bali in August for a holiday with a group of friends from Singapore. Six days later, like the many thousands who travel to the island for fun times, she was heading in a car with her friends to a dance party when police pulled the vehicle over. Inside Michelle's Gucci bag, officers were to allege, they found two pink tablets wrapped in tissue paper. Ecstasy, said police. But Michelle, a model described as having 'the perfect face', allegedly claimed that two friends had given the tablets to her although she didn't know what they were. Her claim was contradicted by police who said that she had purchased the pills in the street for $20 each.

Did police expect to find drugs when they pulled over the car Michelle was in? Major Mardiaz Kusin, an intelligence officer with the Bali drug squad, said the search had been purely routine and random. And he insisted that foreigners were not being targeted, pointing out that four Indonesians had also been arrested with ecstasy that night.

Michelle's arrest sent shock waves among her friends and colleagues in the fashion industry. 'I seriously could not believe it,' Alex Zabotto-Bentley, a fashion stylist on Channel Ten's *Search for a Supermodel* – in which Michelle had competed – told *The Sydney Morning Herald*. 'It's like some horrible, disgusting misunderstanding. She was just a gorgeous girl, really innocent, special and sweet.' Others in the fashion industry also spoke of her sweetness and Michelle's father, Albert, said his daughter's predicament was out of character.

Even so police, who had found no sign of drugs in her system, still charged her with being in possession of psychotropic drugs, which carried a minimum term of 4 years and a maximum of 15. She was jailed pending her court hearing in November, which turned out to be brief, and a conviction. But the prosecution had asked for only a three-month prison term, which meant that she was due for release immediately, having already served that time behind bars. Her lawyer, Ross Hill, said she should never have been arrested or charged, adding that she had never been in trouble with the law before and would now try to rebuild her good name.

Michelle told the three judges that she accepted the guilty verdict, then shook hands with each of them. She told later how terrified she had been. 'From the day of my arrest until the day I was released, I really believed I would spend the next 15 years of my life rotting in an Indonesian prison,' she said.

Many of those caught smuggling drugs into Bali arrive on flights from South-East Asian countries such as Malaysia, Thailand and Vietnam. Anthony Fabian came in during June 2017 looking forward to a relaxed time in Bali, smoking a little marijuana now and again. The 23-year-old Frenchman might have considered the 14 grams of cannabis and a small bag of marijuana seeds would never be detected as he waited in the immigration queue for his entry stamp. He placed his luggage onto the X-ray machine's conveyor belt and the duty officer became suspicious of a shape. When the backpack was opened, Lambert was facing jail time, unless he was found not guilty. His charge started to wend its way through Bali's legal system as he was held up as an example that even the smallest amount of drugs can change the course of a person's life.

Two months after Fabian's arrest a Russian man was sent to jail for 17 years for marijuana offences, although the volume of the drug was massive compared to Fabian's. The 29-year-old Russian, Roman Kalashnikov, was caught at Ngurah Rai Airport after arriving from Kuala Lumpur carrying 2.9 kilograms of hashish, cunningly hidden inside 25 tubes of toothpaste.

Judges are sometimes swayed by a defendant's politeness and it worked this time with Kalashnikov. Judge Partha Bhargawa said the defendant's politeness throughout the court session, his admission of guilt and the fact he had no previous conviction played a part in the sentence, which was three years lighter than the 20 years that prosecutors had requested. The Russian was lucky, for he could have ended up facing the firing squad for trafficking more than one kilogram of a type-one narcotic – ironic for a man whose surname is on one of the world's most common weapons.

Among the prisoners he was to find waiting for him in Kerobokan was South African Brett Savage, part of what might be called the South African connection, and a dead ringer for American actor Tommy Lee Jones.

Savage, now 48, is serving life imprisonment following his arrest at Bali airport in October 2012, when his baggage was inspected and found to be holding more than a quarter of a million dollars' worth of crystal meth, known as 'tik' in South Africa. He was caught in a routine X-ray, when officers noticed what they said was an 'unusual item' in his suitcase.

His sentencing to life imprisonment in May 2012 made him the second South African to receive a long prison term following the jailing earlier in May of 38-year-old Sheila Motsweneng for trafficking 2.5 kilograms of tik, half a kilogram less than Savage's consignment. She was sent to prison for 15 years.

It was not known if Savage and Motsweneng were working together, although their arrests for carrying the same drug from the same country for close to the same amount and almost the same time suggested they were part of a syndicate – and a judge said so when Savage was sentenced.

AsiaOne news reported that presiding judge Komang Wijaya Adhi said Savage was a member of an organised narcotics syndicate that had a wide international network. The prosecution had asked for a 17-year jail sentence so the verdict of life imprisonment had come as a shock to Savage.

'The defendant has committed an unlawful act, which is against the government's programme to eradicate drug trafficking in Indonesia,' said the judge. The court had heard that the drugs Savage tried to bring into Bali were destined to be passed on to an Indonesian woman called Sri Handayani. When she was tracked down and arrested by drug squad officers she said the drugs were in turn to have been delivered to a Nigerian soccer player, Osita Emmanuel Obumneme. Handayani was sentenced to ten years imprisonment, while the Nigerian received seven years.

In South Africa, where Savage, the father of a teenager daughter and son, had worked as a restaurant manager in Johannesburg, his mother, Myra, said the family was devastated at the thought they would never see him again, as they could not afford the fare to fly to Bali.

'He didn't do drugs and he didn't drink so I was shocked to hear he had been arrested in Bali because I didn't even know he was going to Bali,' she said. It appeared that the mother of Savage's children, who lives in Britain, was also unaware of his movements.

His mother said her son received nothing much to eat in Kerobokan prison, just two slices of bread and a banana a day. 'We have to send him money to live and to buy necessities like toiletries. The South African government has not helped. They went to see him once, no-one has been to his court case and the worst is that they did not even let us know that he had been sentenced.'

Drug arrests in Bali receive widespread publicity, yet still the mules and the users try to get through the airport hoping to beat the system. The sentence depends on the intended use of the drugs, with different categories of user, courier and dealer, being examined by judges, dealers typically receiving the maximum: death. But even a minor jail sentence can prove to be miserable for those thrown into jail, where a wrong word, a misunderstood glance, can result in a savage beating from other inmates. And while it is not known how many carriers get through the airport undetected, the arrest of even a small percentage might be thought to be a deterrent to others. But not so. Police have revealed that some drug carriers have 'tested the waters' by carrying harmless material that might look like a drug stash when they have gone on a 'dry run' on an earlier occasion.

Although there is no evidence, it is possible that Singaporean Desmond Goh, an air cabin crew member, had learned of the methods carriers had used to smuggle drugs through the airport. Goh was caught with 1.47 grams of meth and two ecstasy pills in separate plastic sachets when he arrived at the airport in October 2016 – this time on holiday.

'We did a body search and we found the drugs in his wallet,' said Budi Harjanto, the airport's customs chief. 'He planned to send a week of vacation in Bali and consume the drugs, which he bought in Singapore, himself.'

For such a relatively minor offence, Goh was facing a fine and a jail term of between 5 and 15 years. Just four weeks earlier another Singaporean, Muhammad Faliq Nordin, 32, who was working illegally as a DJ in Bali, was caught in a drugs sting operation when he picked up two packages, which arrived separately from the Netherlands, at a post office in Denpasar. The 110.2 grams of crystal meth and 30.3 grams of cocaine had an estimated street value of $10,000.

Bali's drug scene thrives on the island's tourism. Take away the tourists and, experts agree, there will be addicts who remain but the drug trade would largely fall away dramatically. As it is today, pushing a pin into an atlas is likely to strike a country from which a national has arrived with a small stash and got away with it or been caught and charged – or who has purchased drugs from a street pusher.

When they are caught – and there is no bail – arrested people are ordered to put on an orange prisoner uniform in which they are then paraded before local media. The photos make their way around the world, officials hoping the practice will scare others into doing nothing more than leaving their drugs behind and taking a vacation in Bali.

New Zealand senior barrister Craig Tuck agreed that Bali authorities dramatise drug arrests to help them in the fight against narcotics. 'They'll take every opportunity when they catch a foreigner to put them in an orange jumpsuit, put balaclavas on, and [police with] machine guns and tell the local media and the international media just how it rolls. They consider foreigners bringing drugs into the country is colonising the country. It certainly has a lot of detrimental effects on the community and they're responding with pretty brutal tactics including firing squads for some.'

In 2014 Mr Tuck stepped into the defence of a New Zealand man, Antony Glen de Malmanche, who was caught with 1.7 kilograms of meth in his backpack following a flight from Hong Kong – a quantity that would see him led before a firing squad if convicted. Malmanche escaped death, but he was still sentenced to 15 years jail, a term that Mr Tuck later said his client was struggling to comprehend. De Malmanche's legal team had claimed that the bearded 53-year-old was a victim of trafficking, suffered from a mental illness and was vulnerable to brainwashing by online crooks. But chief judge Cening Budiana said de Malmanche 'cannot escape his criminal responsibility and we found no excuse or justification for what he did, so the defendant must be punished.' In addition to the jail sentence the New Zealander was ordered to pay a fine of $390,000.

Three years later, in April 2017, New Zealand woman, 28-year-old Myra Williams, who had been living in Australia, was sentenced to two and a half years jail after a plastic bag containing just 0.43 grams of meth fell out of her pocket at the airport. According to police, she had behaved 'erratically' while waiting to go through immigration and she was led to an office and offered water. But when a customs officer arrived, it was claimed, the plastic bag containing the narcotics fell from her pocket.

The court heard that she had confessed to taking meth, ecstasy and marijuana at a party in Melbourne the night before her flight. She had started using drugs after the death of her mother, she explained. She was found guilty of category one drug abuse for personal use and the sentence she received was six months shorter than that requested by prosecutors – yet much harsher than the punishments imposed on former Reuters correspondent David Fox and the Australian Giuseppe Serafino, who were convicted of the same crime.

So those involved in drugs continue to come and go, receiving varying sentences for the same type of crimes. Some will be 'let off' with a few months or a few years, while others will find themselves on death row. But the message is clear: whoever flies to Bali with drugs in their possession or in their baggage runs a major risk of punishment.

President Widodo has said numerous times that he is determined to stamp out drugs from his country and he was said to have been impressed with the way Philippines President Rodrigo Duterte was going about ridding his nation of the scourge of narcotics – sending out death squads to gun down suppliers, pushers and addicts.

In August 2016, Budi Waseso, chief of Indonesia's National Narcotics Agency, met President Widodo to give him a run-down on an agreement reached among South-East Asian nations to find ways to curtail the circulation of drugs through the region. Mr Waseso assured the President that his agency would continue to look for better ways of eradicating narcotics with the Chinese government and other countries from which drugs allegedly come into Bali and the rest of the country. The President learned that China is a producer of a particular precursor that can be used to manufacture both legal and 'social' drugs. It was the potential of the precursors to be used in making illegal drugs that posed a problem, the regional representatives agreed.

'Modern warfare does not involve firearms,' Mr Waseso told his President. Rather, the lethal weapon is drugs. 'This is what we are trying to combat as this has become a global problem.' Later, Mr Waseso revealed to reporters that the President hoped the drug issue could be resolved in dealing with it in the countries where narcotics were manufactured before they could reach Indonesia.

But with the ongoing arrests and the drugs being offered in the streets, it seems that the President's hopes were easier anticipated than accomplished.

CHAPTER EIGHTEEN

'A VERY BRUTAL MURDER'

It was a gruesome discovery. A farmer heading out into his rice paddy came across the decomposing body of a foreign man in a ditch. It was Tuesday, 21 October 2014, when police, responding to the farmer's call for help, rushed to the rice field between Kuta and Ubud.

The man had a deep wound in his throat – so deep that he had almost been decapitated. It was obvious from a mere glance that someone wanted to be very sure that he was dead. His hands and feet were tied, there were also bruises around the man's mouth, his right cheek and his upper arms, suggesting he had been restrained. Close by, police found a sheet of plastic, a large mat and some bedding that had been used to wrap the body.

'A glance would tell you that this was an execution-style murder,' said Dr Ida Bagus Alit, a member of the police forensic team, based at Sanglah Hospital.

It wasn't long before police knew who the victim was – Robert Kelvin Ellis, 60, a burly, sandy-haired man who held British and Australian passports, and who, with his Balinese wife Noor, ran a luxury villa close to Sanur beach, 25 kilometres from where the body had been found. She was the first to be questioned, before inquiries spread out among the couple's friends and neighbours. Very quickly detectives learned that there had been problems between husband and wife. But could she really have had any involvement in such a terrible crime?

Police suspicions would not go away amid reports that Noor believed Ellis had been cheating on her. They pushed hard but she continued to deny involvement, instead telling officers that she suspected her housemaids and local thugs were responsible for the murder.

Forensic officers combed through the couple's residence and established Ellis had been murdered in the kitchen. Why didn't Noor know about it? She insisted that she had been asleep in a guest room next door to the kitchen and hadn't heard a thing. A post-mortem examination of Ellis's body confirmed that he had indeed died from having his throat slashed and wounds suggested three attempts had been made before his artery was severed.

'Blood would have gone everywhere. It was a very brutal murder, but at least he would then have died quickly,' Dr Alit, at the Sanglah Hospital, was to say later when he confirmed the severity of the cut to Ellis's throat. Dr Alit also confirmed that the bruising on the dead man's arms suggested he had been tied down and would have been unable to defend himself when the brutal attempts to eventually slash his throat were made.

Police inquiries proceeded rapidly. They became convinced that Noor, if not directly involved in her husband's murder, had played a part by arranging it. They took her to police headquarters where she finally agreed that she had simply asked her housemaids to organise a group of men to give her husband a hard time – a talking to, was the way she put it – but insisted he should not by harmed.

'I had to take these measures because he was holding onto our money. He was cheating on me, too,' she told police. Officers wanted to know, of course, why it had taken a call from a rice farmer for them to be alerted to the death of Ellis; why hadn't she reported him missing? She admitted that she had realised he was dead when she was wakened by a knock on the door and a man telling her, 'Ibu (Ma'am), the job is done.'

She had then gone into the kitchen where she saw her blood-soaked husband's body on the floor. At that point, the men responsible told her that she had to get rid of the body. 'I don't want this,' she claims she said, but she alleged the killers told her to do it 'or we'll kill you, too.'

'How am I going to do this?' she said she had asked and she was given instructions on where to drive with the body and dump it. 'It was in the middle of nowhere,' her lawyer, Nyoman Wisnu Yasa said after learning Noor's version.

Two housemaids confessed that they knew about the plot by a wife who police said had felt 'embittered' because of his alleged money hoarding and his cheating on her with other women.

Badung police chief Komang Suartana said his officers had established that Noor paid one of her maid's boyfriends, Adreanus Ngongo, also known as Arli, along with other men to kill Ellis for the price of $14,000. With such a large number ganging up against him, he would have had no hope of defending himself. Most of the money would be paid after the murder, it had been arranged. One of the maids was ordered to help in dumping the body while a second had the job of cleaning up the blood in the kitchen.

With the murder of the British-Australian villa owner apparently clearly established, police weighed up the charges they would lay. Murder alone would carry a jail sentence of 15 years, but if it was planned and a conviction obtained the maximum penalty would be death. Although police had Noor, two maids and Arli in custody, they had learned that four others were involved in the murder – and it was likely that at least two of them had already fled Bali for the neighbouring large island of Java. 'Wherever they are, we'll hunt them down,' said a police spokesman.

As is often the case, the tragedy had wide reaching effects. In Perth, where Mr Ellis had lived with Noor before they had moved to Sanur, the couple's student sons, Jon and Peter Ellis, released a statement saying their father had been a huge influence on their lives and they had been completely devastated by his death.

'The circumstances surrounding the death of our father is something we are still trying to come to terms with at this moment. We are fortunately surrounded by friends and family,' they said.

In the meantime, rumours continued to swirl about Ellis's troubled relationship with Noor. A friend of the couple told Fairfax Media that he spent a lot of his time in Jakarta, the Indonesian capital, where he had an apartment.

Ellis was also said to have built up enemies after infuriated contractors who were building a motel for him when he told them they were not doing a very good job, and they were having problems getting money from him.

In the days before Ellis's body was found, his wife phoned their son Peter in Australia when he was about to start working for Australia Post. She told him, 'I'm proud of you, well done.'

'It was really motherly stuff. She was being a loving mother and behind the scenes she was plotting the murder of my father,' said Peter. He recalled that after learning of the discovery of the body of a white man in a field, his girlfriend called him to say she thought it was his dad. He desperately tried to get in touch with his mother.

'She wasn't answering calls, which is bizarre, because she had her phone with her all the time. At the time I thought something might have happened to her as well.'

Police charged Noor with premeditated murder, meaning that she would go on trial defending herself against receiving the maximum penalty – death by firing squad. When her case got under way it was astonishingly revealed by Any Aryani, a lawyer representing her sons, that she was claiming to be of 'another religion', so she would not lose her inheritance. Her husband was said to have an extensive business empire worth an estimated $30 million across Indonesia, Australia and New Zealand.

Along with her claims that her husband had neglected her, withheld sex and denied her money to which she was entitled, she stated that her religion was Hindu, despite official documents saying she was a Muslim. According to Indonesian family law, if a Muslim woman is convicted of her husband's murder, she loses her rights to benefit from it.

Miss Any told Australian Associated Press that 'if Noor thinks "I killed, I've been punished, but my inheritance rights remain", well that's not possible. We have prepared for that. As soon as the court states Noor is guilty of killing her husband, we will take legal measures that will ensure Noor will not get even the smallest bit of Bob's fortune.'

The time eventually came for the man who cut Ellis's throat to give his evidence. Urbanus Yohanes Ghoghi, who was also facing the death penalty, told the court that he and four other men played a part in the killing. At first, they had tried to suffocate him with a pillow, which Noor had given to one of the men, but the businessman had fought back. It was then that one of the men, Martin, handed Ghoghi a kitchen knife, which he used to slash Ellis's throat.

Next, Noor Ellis produced a sheet of plastic to wrap her husband's body in and that night she gave one of the men $5000 to split between the group of killers. They were promised more, later.

Further grim details relayed to the court revealed that Noor had called a meeting prior to the murder, when she had given the order to kill her husband. 'Mrs Noor said that when killing Mr Bob, don't use a sharp weapon,' Ghoghi told the court. 'Close his nose and mouth with a pillow only. To be neat, basically.'

Noor was ordered to take the stand as a witness in the trials of the two men who had been caught. When Judge Beslin Sihombing asked her where her husband was now, she replied, 'In heaven.'

And when the judge wanted to know who gave the order to have him murdered, she admitted, 'Probably me.'

Why had she given the order? 'For a long time, he hadn't given me sufficient [money]. He even took the money for my kids' schooling. Because his attitude didn't change, I couldn't stand it anymore. Once I asked for divorce but he didn't want to. He said we should just go on, in our own way.' She also claimed that she had been 'possessed by an evil spirit' when she played her role in her husband's murder.

For her two sons, emotions were running high. While they wanted justice for the death of their father, they realised that it could also mean the death of their mother. The dilemma resulted in them being unable to sit in the court while Noor's case proceeded. Instead, Peter's girlfriend, Maddison McNeil, agreed to go to the court – she had known Noor as a second mother from vacations in Bali and from a visit by the Ellis couple to Maddison's home.

In the grounds of the Denpasar court house, Noor, in handcuffs, told Maddison, 'I love you. Pray for me.'

It was hard for Maddison. 'She's still my boyfriend's mum,' she said. 'She's still Noor. But she'll never be the same and we'll never be the same.'

At the end of May 2015, the time approached for the court to hand down its verdict.

Bob Ellis's brother David, who also has an Indonesian wife, recalled how Bob had told him that if his marriage ever broke up he wouldn't get married again. They were, said David, regarded as role models for successful mixed-race marriages. 'I've always liked Noor,' he said. 'There were narcissistic elements to her personality, but she was an easy person to talk to. I enjoyed her company. If they had divorced, I would have been happy to go and see her sometimes if she was living down the road.'

Noor's reference to being possessed by an evil spirit was no surprise to David. She was, he recalled, 'right into the dark side of the occult', with her admitting that she had once tried to place a voodoo curse on her husband. David told *The Sydney Morning Herald*, 'Noor was a bit like a crackhead down a deep hole. She probably got so angry and so vengeful she didn't even think about the proper way of doing things.'

It had come as a shock when prosecutors asked for Noor to be sentenced to just 15 years jail, when the maximum could have been death by firing squad for a premeditated murder. David had found it hard to believe. 'In Indonesia, when you are a drug trafficker you are a mass murderer. When you slit someone's throat you are just killing one person.'

Noor's defence team fought hard to prove that she was innocent, despite her confession that she had ordered the murder. But her lawyers told the court that she did not give the order for her husband to be murdered and the pillow and a towel she had given to one of the attackers had not caused the stabbing wounds that killed him, said her lawyer, Ketut Suwiga Dauh. 'She only instructed to have her problems with her husband handled.' Robert Ellis, the court was told by Noor's defence, was a womaniser who deprived his wife of money from their joint business enterprises.

With just a few days to go before the verdict, Ellis's son Peter, who was in Bali with family members, said there was no point in him returning in the future if his father was not around.

'Whenever I come here, I expect Dad to be at the airport and give me a big hug,' he said. He was a cheerful man who knew the names of all the street vendors he would see on his 6 am walks. 'He had a characteristic way of standing, laughing and talking.'

On 10 June 2015, the judges announced their verdict. And it was a shock, even though prosecutors had already suggested a jail sentence, not execution. The judges agreed that Noor Ellis would not be sentenced to death – but neither was she to receive the 15 years imprisonment prosecutors had asked for. Instead, she would go to jail for just 12 years.

Bob Ellis's family were stunned. In a tweet, Peter Ellis described the verdict as a 'disgrace'.

And in a statement, he said, 'Today we heard the verdict…and we as a family are extremely disappointed with the outcome of 12 years. We would have expected a sentence of at least 20 years for the brutal premeditated murder of our father. For the verdict to be a sentence of only 12 years is unjust not only for us as a family but Indonesia in general. We are still coming to terms with this sentencing decision and would like an appeal from the prosecutor.'

As well as criticising the judgement, Peter said the family was disgusted at Noor's claims against his father – claims of affairs and denying her money. 'She had fabricated them in order to defend herself,' he said. The brothers said they had disowned their mother and they never wanted to see 'the murderer' again.

Why had the judges given such an unexpectedly light sentence? Presiding judge Anak Agung Anom Wirakanta spoke of a bad relationship with her husband for the past 11 years and made reference to her regretting her crime, she had confessed, had no criminal record and had suffered mentally from the murder.

Meanwhile two of the killers, Urbanus Yoh Ghoghi and Yohanes Sairokodu, also received prison terms of 12 years. Other hitmen were also rounded up, two being arrested on nearby Sumba Island after a dramatic police chase during which they fired at police with poison arrows, before police bullets in the legs brought them down.

Bali has its beauty – but the dark side is fearful.

CHAPTER NINETEEN

SCHAPELLE FREED, BUT LINDSAY STAYS ON DEATH ROW

Bali's beauty lies in its beaches, its fantastic sunsets, exotic meals and the charm of its friendly people. The dark side is often brought in by strangers abusing what they mistakenly believe is the naivety of the Balinese by defiantly smuggling (or trying to) drugs onto the island, drinking too much, fighting, and riding recklessly on rented motor scooters. And in the case of Heather Mack and her boyfriend Tommy Schaefer, and the Bob Ellis killers, committing murders that shocked the world.

Although Bob Ellis's wife Noor was a Muslim until she announced she had changed her religion to Hindu to join the majority of Balinese, she showed with her plot to kill her husband that it was not just foreigners who are capable of wickedness. The fact that she was also able to easily enlist the services of a group of local men, ready and willing to attack and kill him, demonstrated that evil could be found among the island's very own inhabitants. The drug pushers, too, are not without blame, collecting narcotics from various sources and seeking out gullible tourists.

Despite her bizarre behaviour, in which she seemingly confessed to being solely responsible for her mother's murder, Heather Mack was taking good care of her daughter Stella in Kerobokan prison. But she was aware time was running out. When the child reached the age of two she would have to be passed to a local family.

That time came in March 2017, when an expatriate woman who had supported Heather almost from the day she was arrested, came to the prison to take the little girl away. It was a heartbreaking moment. 'I know she has to go, but it's tearing me apart,' said Heather on the morning of her saying goodbye to Stella.

In the hours leading up to the separation, fellow women prisoners held a happy two-years-old birthday party for the child, slicing up a chocolate cake topped with fruit and nuts in the cell they all shared.

Heather, by then aged 21 and with 8 years to still to serve, shed tears as she repeated that parting with her daughter was very hard, but she was grateful that she had been allowed to keep Stella with her for the first two years of her life.

'In the prison she has been surrounded by love every day of her life — she's a star among the other women,' said Heather, revealing that fears expressed by the other women that a baby in their cell would be disruptive were unfounded.

'Everything outside prison will be very strange to her now but I want her to stay in Bali and be close so she can visit me as often as possible. She's a little girl and she needs her mother, whatever I've done. I'm so relieved that Stella isn't going back to America to live with Tommy's mother, which is what his mother had been trying to arrange. I couldn't bear it if I was here and Stella was in America. By the time I got back, I'd be a stranger to her. At least now she'll be brought to visit me from time to time.'

Inmates also spoke fondly of not only the child but of her mother. One prisoner noted that in the 'outside world' children are sat down in front of a TV set by their mothers, but with no TV in prison, cell life could only have been good for the child's first two years.

While Heather and the other women prisoners were happy that the young girl would be living with a local family, Schaefer made it known he was totally in disagreement that she should be remaining in Bali. 'This is wrong!' he shouted from the men's side of Kerobokan. 'Stella doesn't belong here in Bali. She's my child and I say that she should be with my mother in America. I'm American, Heather is American and Stella is American. Why is she being allowed to stay in Bali?'

The drama ended another chapter in the shocking story of the Body in the Suitcase, but there was talk around Bali in the days that followed the handing over of Stella to the local woman that it would not end there. There had been many twists and turns and the belief in the cafes, hotels and homes of Bali was that there would be more to come, particularly as Heather Mack, on her release, would apparently be able to get her hands on the \$US1.63 million fortune of the mother she had murdered. By then Heather's daughter, who would be aged ten, could be assured of a life without wanting for anything.

When Heather was originally jailed, among the prisoners she met was Schapelle Corby, who had endured an emotional roller-coaster with appeals lodged, allowed, rejected until finally it was agreed that she would be granted parole on 7 February 2014. She would by then have served nine years in Kerobokan, during which time she would have been treated for depression, which resulted in her being admitted to hospital.

While Schapelle's parole meant she could finally walk from the prison, strict conditions were imposed on her. She had to remain in Bali and abide by a number of rules drawn up by the corrections bureau, to whom she also had to check in monthly. In addition, she had to agree not to use or distribute drugs – a risk, after all the years in jail she was hardly likely to take – dress neatly and appropriately to the approval of officials and allow the authorities to carry out checks without warning on the home of her Balinese brother-in-law, where she would initially be staying.

In the first few weeks of her release she was photographed swimming off Kuta Beach, a plumper figure than the young woman who had arrived at the airport. She became visibly annoyed at the paparazzi, who were snapping shots of her whenever she appeared in public. She did her best to avoid being pictured by remaining mostly indoors. 'In a way she's gone from one prison to another,' said a nearby cafe owner.

But Schapelle finally got her revenge on the media who were waiting to join her on her eventual 'absolute freedom' flight back to Australia in May 2017. Word spread that she had been booked on a Virgin flight (a photo of her boarding pass had even been circulated on social media) but at the last minute she and sister Mercedes boarded a Malindo flight to Brisbane, leaving most writers and photographers on the wrong plane. As for photos of her in Bali, aside from blurry snatched shots of her in dark glasses and a headscarf, she did most of the photographing, posting pictures of herself saying goodbye to her pet puppy dogs and family and friends.

Then in Australia, the sisters left the airport in a convoy of cars which split up and headed in three different directions: to a hotel, to Schapelle's mother's house and the third towards the Gold Coast. Schapelle managed to successfully lose all her followers and set up an Instagram account showing herself enjoying her freedom, which attracted more than 100,000 followers in less than 24 hours. It resulted in numerous messages of support, one writer commenting, 'You're an incredibly strong, brave woman. You could probably teach a lot of people a thing or two about resilience.'

In the days that followed, Schapelle played cat and mouse with the searching media, taunting everyone with social media posts that showed her in a number of exotic locations, believed to be in north Queensland. Just where, she wasn't saying.

Among the notable prisoners Schapelle had greeted from time to time in Kerobokan was a middle-aged English woman who looked for all the part like someone's grandmother. Schapelle was already 7 years into her original 20-year sentence when they brought Lindsay Sandiford, then aged 56, into the prison in 2012. Like Schapelle, she had been caught red-handed with drugs in her luggage, but unlike Schapelle she made no attempt to hide the fact that she knew they were there.

A former legal secretary originally from Redcar in North Yorkshire, Lindsay had arrived at Bali airport on a flight from Bangkok on 19 May 2012 and in what was described as a 'routine luggage search' customs officers found 4.8 kilograms of cocaine in the lining of her suitcase. This was a massive haul, worth $2.4 million.

What on earth was a plumpish Englishwoman doing, trying to smuggle such a large amount of narcotics into Bali, where she would have known that she could be sentenced to death if caught? Narcotics officers led her to an interview room where she told them she had been forced to carry the cocaine by a criminal gang in the UK who threatened to harm members of her family if she didn't act as a drugs mule.

She admitted, too, that she was to pass the drugs on to a British syndicate living in Bali. Police who were called in to the interview room raised their eyes in surprise; they did not know about this group. They wanted to know everything – and assured her that her co-operation would help her receive a lenient sentence. Just for the record, however, they needed a photo of her with the drugs and with grinning officers surrounding her, she was ordered to sit with the large pile in front of her as she lowered her head and tried to hide her face behind her hand.

I followed Lindsay's trail in the wake of her arrest from the airport to a small hotel used frequently by police when dealing with potential witnesses.

She was given time to ponder her options, for while she had told police her family would be harmed if the drugs did not reach their destination, she was well aware her own life would be in danger if she failed to co-operate with police and judges learned of her failure to tell all.

Under the gaze of undercover officers posing as tourists, Lindsay spent 12 hours wandering around the hotel's exotic gardens, working out what she should do. She had been put up in a $38-a-night deluxe room and sat down in the small restaurant area where she ordered a bowl of nasi goreng. She made up her mind – she would tell the police everything.

She named a British antique dealer, Julian Ponder, 43, who was living in Bali, and his partner, Rachel Dougall, 38. Arrangements were made by Lindsay to contact Ponder, as well as another Briton, Paul Beales, at the hotel. When they turned up, Lindsay passed the drugs, disguised as a present in pink wrapping paper, to Ponder. Police swooped, arresting him on suspicion of drug trafficking. Police then raided the luxury villa, complete with its own swimming pool, where Ponder was living with Rachel Dougall, and arrested her.

At the villa, surrounded by rice paddies in the Tabanan district of Bali, household staff told me of the luxury lifestyle enjoyed by Ponder and Dougall, with champagne parties being held for other expatriates. But for local people, their wealthy lives and aloof attitude had been a source of intrigue, resulting in them being nicknamed the King and Queen of Bali. Many wondered how the couple were able to afford the $1500-a-week rent, given that they seemed to have no occupations. Another local person said the couple, who had moved to Bali from Brighton four years earlier, had never revealed details of their secretive business to their household staff. They would spend days behind the walls of the villa and not mix with those local people who were not their immediate friends.

When police raided the villa, they revealed they had found drugs hidden in cigarette boxes, discovering a total of 48.94 grams of cocaine, adding to their suspicions that they had cracked open a syndicate. But Ponder was determined to fight for his innocence, his lawyer telling ITV news, 'Julian Ponder believes 100 per cent that he was trapped by Lindsay. He said he thought the gift-wrapped packages bearing the words "Enjoy Sweet Candy" were sweets for his little daughter.'

'She knew my daughter was going to be six shortly after her arrival,' Ponder was quoted as saying. 'Having been caught, she aided the police surveillance and brought the cocaine to me wrapped as if it was a present for my daughter. I never touched the drugs.'

Meanwhile Paul Beales, also pointed out by Lindsay, protested his innocence from his remand cell, which he was sharing with seven other men. Police claimed, however, that they had found hashish at his house. 'This is a nightmare,' he said. 'I'm not involved with drugs. I don't know what I'm doing here. Scared? Of course I am. I have a flat bit of cardboard to sit on and we have one mattress that we share.'

But it was Lindsay Sandiford who was the prize catch. Bali journalists who covered the courts said there was no doubt that she would avoid the death penalty because she was telling the police everything she knew. Many years in prison was the most likely sentence, it was agreed.

As the days went by, Lindsay's background emerged. She had been living in more recent times in Cheltenham, Gloucestershire, where she worked in the management side of a legal firm. Separated from her husband, she was renting a house but she was evicted after failing to pay her rent. A few months before her Bali arrest, she moved to India.

Like so many other Westerners brought before the courts in Bali, Lindsay and the other Britons had to wait as the months rolled by with delays and remands. And it was some relief to her to hear prosecutors at an initial hearing tell the judges that she should be given a low, 15-year sentence if convicted because of her age and her co-operation during investigations.

In the meantime, Paul Beales and Rachel Dougall's cases went ahead, with Beales being jailed for four years for possessing 3.1 grams of cannabis and Dougall being sent to prison for 12 months for failing to report a crime to the authorities. What police and the prosecution regarded as the 'big fish' in a drug syndicate – Lindsay Sandiford and Julian Ponder – still had to go through the courts. Sandiford had been charged with drugs trafficking, while Ponder was charged with conspiring to import, smuggle and exchange drugs and being part of a drug syndicate.

Back in the UK, it was revealed that Lindsay had given birth to her first son, Lewis, in 1988 followed two years later by Eliot, who was said to have learning difficulties. She married the boys' father, Nicholas, in

London in 1994 but when the marriage broke down Lindsay moved from Redcar, Teeside, in the north of England, to Cheltenham, in the West Country. Neighbours told reporters that Lindsay was 'the neighbour from hell' who would regularly hold late-night parties. Even so, a friend said she never would have expected her to become involved in smuggling drugs. 'She was always a party girl, but I didn't think she was capable of this,' said the friend.

When the trial finally got under way, prosecutors told the court that Lindsay Sandiford had met Rachel Dougall and Paul Beales at a hotel in Bangkok on 17 May 2012, where it was arranged she would carry the cocaine to Bali. Two days later, on her arrival, she was caught out. She repeated to the court what she had been saying all along, that her sons were being threatened and she had to go ahead with the drug plan. Her lawyers argued, too, that she had been suffering from mental health problems.

In her own witness statement Lindsay told the court, 'I would like to begin by apologising to the Republic of Indonesia and the Indonesian people for my involvement. I would never have become involved in something like this but the lives of my children were in danger and I felt I had to protect them.'

The court also heard a statement from her son, read out by her lawyer. The statement said, 'I love my mother very much and have a very close relationship with her. I know that she would do anything to protect me. I cannot imagine what I would do if she was sentenced to death in relation to these charges.'

He added that he believed she had been forced to carry the drugs following a disagreement over rent money, which she had paid on his behalf. The statement is understood to have been made before prosecutors told the court that they wanted Lindsay jailed for 15 years.

It seemed that a prison sentence, rather than death, was virtually a 'done deal' for the British woman, a likelihood enhanced by Dr Jennifer Fleetwood, a criminology lecturer at Kent University, and an expert on women in the international drugs trade.

She told the court that Lindsay was an ideal target for drug traffickers, who would look for someone who was vulnerable. She added that having examined extracts from Lindsay's medical records she knew she had a history of mental health issues which might have made her a target for manipulation, threats and coercion.

As she had expected, given her co-operation with the authorities and implicating herself, Lindsay was formally convicted of trafficking on 19 December 2012. She then had a wait of several weeks for the expected maximum sentence of 15 years, requested by prosecutors, to be handed down.

Julian Ponder, meanwhile, was cleared of drug smuggling but found guilty of possessing narcotics when he appeared in court in January 2013. He was sentenced to six years imprisonment.

On 23 January, Lindsay sat before the panel of judges in a white blouse as the sentence was read out. It started out badly.

Judge Amser Simanjuntak, heading the panel, said there were no mitigating circumstances in her favour. She had damaged Bali's reputation as a tourist destination and undermined Indonesia's fight against drugs. A second judge, Komang Wijya Adi, said they had been influenced by several factors, including what was viewed as Lindsay's lack of remorse. Then came the sentencing:

Death by firing squad.

Gasps rang out around the crowded court. Someone sitting near Lindsay heard her whisper to herself 'No, no,' before she put a hand to her eyes. She was ushered to her feet, her face lined with shock, and led from the courtroom to be driven to Kerobokan jail.

Her equally stunned lawyers announced immediately that she would appeal, knowing that the process could take several years. If they failed, those 'several years' would be spent in a prison cell with no freedom until she was shot dead.

'It's not going to happen,' said a British tourist who had managed to secure a seat in the court. 'Indonesia is never going to tie a British grandmother to a stake and gun her down. Never.'

The British Embassy in Jakarta issued a statement saying the UK remained strongly opposed to the death penalty 'in all circumstances', adding that the Embassy was in touch with the British government to discuss the best way to provide Lindsay with ongoing good legal representation.

What happened in Bali with the imposing of the death penalty brought widespread condemnation in the UK – at least in official circles. There were also opposite views from members of the public who said the convicted grandmother deserved whatever punishment she received because no excuse was good enough to explain drug trafficking

Her MP in Cheltenham, Martin Horwood, told of his shock, saying that the 'days of the death penalty ought to be past. This is not the way that a country that now values democracy and human rights should really be behaving.' And the charity Reprieve, which is against capital punishment, announced it had taken up her case, insisting that Lindsay was not a drug kingpin. She didn't even have the money to pay for a lawyer or to pay the travel costs for defence witnesses. In fact, said Reprieve, there wasn't enough money for her to pay for a reliable supply of food and water. More to the point, the group said that Lindsay had co-operated fully with the Indonesian authorities but had been sentenced to death while the gang operating in the UK, in Thailand and Indonesia remained free to target other vulnerable people.

When Lindsay was sentenced, there had been no executions in Indonesia for five years, but a month after she was told she would be executed the country's Attorney General, Basrief Arief, said it was his intention to resume capital punishment by shortening the length of the appeals process, which he considered had brought about a delay in executions. Five weeks later a Malawian drug trafficker was executed by firing squad. There was another death a month later, in April, but it was by natural causes; Amser Simanjuntak, one of the judges who had sentenced Lindsay was found dead at his home from a heart attack.

What was to follow as the gates of Kerobokan prison clanged behind her was a nightmare of legal efforts to avoid being put to death. While she had seven days to lodge an appeal against the sentence, an initial letter of appeal, drawn up by diplomats, was rejected because it should have been filed from the prison. But finally, five days after the sentence, the appeal request was received from Lindsay. Then followed a further two weeks in which she had to file a more detailed appeal. Ahead of her she knew there were still several avenues of hope – appealing to the High Court, the Supreme Court and finally a direct appeal for clemency to the President.

Adding strength to her fight for her life was a claim by Britain's Foreign and Commonwealth Office that police had denied Lindsay sleep and had threatened her with a gun following her arrest. The document stated that police had 'violated Lindsay Sandiford's fundamental rights under international laws and the Indonesian constitution', and it went on to say her punishment was disproportionate to the crime she had committed and had failed to consider her co-operation with the authorities. But the first appeal was denied and a new batch of legal documents was drawn up for the next round of the battle.

A fight on her behalf was also going on in London, a fight for funds to pay top lawyers. But her hopes of winning funds through an appeal to the High Court were dismissed. Her supporters in the UK appealed that dismissal, but failed again. Lindsay agreed to a written interview with BBC Radio 5 Live in which she said that failing to receive financial help from the government was tantamount to the UK condoning the death penalty.

She spoke from the jail to the *Mail on Sunday* through intermediaries, dramatically announcing that, 'I would rather have the death sentence than a life sentence. I don't want to get old and decrepit in here…at least a bullet is quick.' She reportedly went on to say, 'Telling the truth doesn't help here because you just get the death sentence…I helped the Indonesian police. The next person who gets caught isn't going to say anything.'

With her appeals lost and her plea for mercy to the President in the balance, Lindsay spent her days knitting in her cell, declining to join in with other female prisoners whenever there was a national day of celebration when they were allowed to dance on the lawn. Her sixtieth birthday passed and then her sixty-first, at the end of June 2017.

A Facebook page, run for her by a group called Justice and Fairness for Lindsay Sandiford, carried her thanks a few days later, on 4 July. In a post to her friends and supporters she wrote:

> Thank you to everyone for your kind wishes for my 61st birthday last weekend. I had a thoroughly enjoyable day with visits from some dear friends, a delicious cake and messages from my family and supporters from around the world.
>
> I was immensely touched by all your warm thoughts and I would like

to add a heartfelt thank-you to the wonderful governor of the women's prison here for making the small celebration possible. I would like you all to know that I am keeping well and continuing to work and teach other women on various handicrafts.

In the meantime, keep me in your thoughts and thank you all again for your friendship and support. Warm regards, Lindsay.

Among the items she had made were woollen animals, laid out under the title: The Human Zoo. Was this a not-so-subtle reminder to the world that she too was caged?

CHAPTER TWENTY

BALI 'SEX' LIFE

Bali beach boys have the pick of foreign women. Bali women have the pick of foreign men. Somewhere in between are the lady boys. Just like in Thailand's Pattaya, they play a role in Bali's sex life, targeting tourists who are either too naive to know the 'women' aren't what they look like or the tourists who are too drunk to care.

Meanwhile the beach boys – who despise being called gigolos – hang around Kuta, while Bali's 'ladies of the night' can be found just about anywhere that single male tourists can be found. Take Lily, which you can guarantee is not her real name, who approached me while I was enjoying a Bintang in a fish restaurant a few streets back from Kuta Beach. It had the day's catch laid out on a slab near the entrance and there was no doubt that in Lily's eyes I was a Western fish to fry. I'd heard all the usual lines in South-East Asia but Lily, with her low-slung blouse, pink shorts and a tattoo of a butterfly on her thigh, came up with a new one.

'Excuse me, I'm looking for my friend,' she purred. 'She said she would be here. Have you seen her? She has blonde hair and she's wearing a black dress.'

'Blonde hair?' I asked.

She knew what I meant and pointed out that her 'friend' had had it like that for a long time.

'Haven't seen her,' I said, taking another swig of the male tourist's friend.

Hardly had I put the dark green bottle down, when she came up with another step forward on the original lines front. 'Okay, well, I suppose I should wait here for her, somewhere.'

'If you're looking for her and she said she'd be here, that's all you can do.'

She now edged right up to the table, that butterfly fluttering close to the remnants of my fish dinner. 'Can I sit here and wait for her…for a little while.'

I kept my sigh to myself. 'Sure, go ahead,' I said, aware where this was leading. The next line was going to be along the lines of 'Would you like to buy me a drink?'

'Would you like to buy me a drink?' she said, flashing her eyes. 'My name's Lily.'

'Hello Lily. And look, Lily, I'll buy you a drink or whatever, but—' and now it was my turn, 'I've been waiting here, too, for my friend, who has now probably gone to another place that he likes. So, I'll head off. What was it you wanted to drink, anyway?'

'It's okay,' she said. 'My friend probably isn't coming now.'

And Lily went her way and, after paying my bill, I went mine. Now that was a cool approach. So much smoother than the old 'What your name?' bang, straight-in-there approach of the nightclubs and bars.

Just as the tourism industry has grown in Bali, so has the number of prostitutes, mostly young women who through poverty and poor education have been able to find only menial work. The most recent official figures issued in 2016 from Bali's Provincial Health Office reveal that the island has at least 6000 commercial sex workers. And with that number, said the medical experts, came the worrying claim that more than half were HIV positive. The Bali AIDS Commission reported as far back as 2010 that only 40 per cent of women they had surveyed admitted they insisted their clients used protection.

Today, sex workers in Bali are found mostly in the popular tourist areas of Kuta, Legian, Seminyak, Nusa Dua and Sanur, with Sanur being described by locals as Massage City, due to the numbers of parlours offering varying types of sexual satisfaction.

A locally-based website, Bali Orti, gave some detailed advice about the sex industry in beachside Sanur. 'Balinese girls are beautiful girls,' it gushed. 'Graceful, and polite, friendly and smiling.'

Few would disagree with that sentiment, but the site then went on to point out that the image of the perfect Balinese woman had been tainted by the prostitution industry, which was prolific, particularly in the 'prostitution centre of Sanur. It is no secret that in the Sanur area there are many places of prostitution.'

In its written broken English, Bali Orti continued:

> Very easy to find a place of prostitution in Sanur, Bali. Simply by looking at the house number. If the number of houses in Sanur at the end with the letter X-XX-XXX, assured the house is a place of protitusi in Sanur, Bali.
>
> However, do not expect to easily obtain a Balinese woman prostitute. Prostitutes in Sanur, Bali, mostly immigrant girl from the island of Java. The prostitute came to Bali in the hope of greater earnings in Bali. They are the target of foreign tourists, are willing to pay dearly for them. Therefore, local people paid by foreign tourists can reach 20 times higher…Balinese woman very hard to find in place of prostitution in Sanur, Bali.

However, whether the women were locals or imports from neighbouring Java, they started moving in large numbers into the capital Denpasar at the start of the year 2000, claiming the main tourist areas were 'too crowded' by people in the same profession.

So, was my friend with the butterfly thigh a Javanese import? Do the ladies from Java look any different from those born and raised in Bali? I couldn't tell – and I doubt whether any of the other men Lily met that night after she had approached me in the fish restaurant could tell, or give a damn, either.

Officially, prostitution in Bali and throughout Indonesia is a crime, 'a crime against decency and morality.' Yet it is officially tolerated, perhaps because there just aren't enough police to round up all the working women who would simply end up back on the streets and in the bars and hotels once they paid a nominal fine. For those pulling in a good weekly wage, being fined is just part of the job. An investigation by the *Jakarta Post* found that high-end prostitutes in Jakarta could earn up to $4000 a month and while most women 'on the game' in Bali would not earn anything like that, they still make more than an everyday job would bring in.

It's reputed to be the world's oldest profession and in Bali, before what is today's Indonesia was colonised, while kings in Java had their concubines, the kings of Bali allowed widows who had no means of support to prostitute themselves. The women did what they had to do to survive.

But not all the girls and women who are ready to sleep with strangers necessarily demand money. A category known as 'good girls' might simply want a good time with dinner and drinks before joining her tourist escort back at his hotel. There is often no difficulty in a lonely male tourist finding a girl to accompany him because she will probably find him first, then make her intentions clear. Others will work through a pimp, who could even be a taxi driver who will ask a tourist if he wants a girl, man, boy, girl. And sadly, when he refers to boys and girls, that's exactly what he means, for children, usually from poor families, are offered out for abuse.

The children are targets for paedophiles who fly in from around the world. Many have taken their chances in other South-East Asian countries such as Thailand and Cambodia and have had to leave in a hurry with the authorities on their tail, only to end up in Bali.

By a bizarre coincidence, a little over a year after the wife of expatriate Bob Ellis was sent to jail for his murder, another man called Bob Ellis was on his way to prison for 15 years after being convicted of persuading children to commit an indecent act.

The white-bearded, 70-year-old Australian insisted in court he did not deserve to be imprisoned that long because he wondered if it meant he would die in jail for a crime that was 'not a serious thing' because he had paid the youngsters generously. What he had done was sexually abuse 11 girls who were all under the age of 18 in the 12 months up to 2015. In addition to the 15 years, he was fined the equivalent of $200,000, and if he couldn't pay it he would have to serve a further six months imprisonment.

Judges in Bali take a dim view of criminals who receive widespread publicity, and this particular Bob Ellis was told he had damaged the island's image as a tourist destination, which could lead to a decrease in income. An anti-paedophile activist, former Victorian police officer Glen Hulley, in a social media message to Ellis, wrote:

> You are a vile, despicable human being who shows no sign of remorse for his actions. It's offensive that you continue to portray to the court and the media that you are some caring old man who was just helping some poor children, whom you claim have been paid for their 'inconvenience' and that they love and miss you and that they don't want to see you punished.

We can go back many years to find that child-sex perverts were active in

Bali, men of all ages and professions who believed that the children there were easy targets.

Former Australian diplomat William Brown thought so, but the law caught up with him when he was arrested in 2003 for sexually abusing two boys aged 13 and 15. As his trial proceeded, the child protection group Child Wise claimed there had been an increase in the number of foreign paedophiles in Bali following the Bali bombings, possibly because some children had lost parents, and because there was general chaos in the weeks and months that followed and the predators were able to move about virtually unnoticed.

Luh Ketut Suryani, a professor of psychiatry at a Denpasar University, agreed that Bali, being a popular tourist destination, could present as a safe haven for paedophiles looking for young victims.

Another Bali psychiatrist, Cokorda Bagus Jaya Lesmana, said that in many cases paedophiles showed 'polite and generous traits. They make their approach slowly, helping out the poor. After they feel secure, they start to harass.'

Brown threw a tantrum in court when he was sentenced to 13 years imprisonment and complained bitterly to his lawyer that he had been unjustly treated by the court. But he never saw out his long imprisonment; a few days after he was sentenced he was found hanging in his cell. He had strung himself up to a ventilation grate around midnight using a metre-long cord cut from his mattress with scissors found in his cell. He hadn't even left a suicide note.

Exactly ten years after Brown hanged himself, a Dutch paedophile was sentenced to three years in a court in Singaraja, in northern Bali, for abusing four children, despite the victims later revoking their testimonies, claiming they had been pressured by investigators to point accusing fingers at Jan Jacobus Vogel. During his trial, dozens of villagers from a hamlet on the north coast came to the court carrying banners declaring 'Free Vogel, He is Innocent'. And in bizarre scenes after the verdict was announced, the Dutchman was cheered like a hero by the villagers, some of whom even wept.

It was also in Singaraja, in 2009, that an Australian retired accountant, 62-year-old Philip Grandfield, was sentenced to eight years in jail for sex with teenage boys, and expressed gratitude for the sentence, having feared he would be sentenced to death. 'I'm very happy,' he declared. 'I'm very happy…I thought I might be executed.' In his defence he said he had relationships with boys because he did not realise they were under-age.

A female judge, Sida Aryani, dismissed his excuse, describing his actions with the children as 'lewd', adding he had destroyed the boys' futures and created unease in the community. Following his imprisonment, child protection groups spoke out against foreign men who moved in on children of poor families living in remote villages. They reported that there was an increasing number of paedophiles from Europe, the US and Australia who were travelling to Bali to abuse children.

In July 2007 no less than 485 foreigners had been prevented from entering Indonesia in the previous 12 months on the basis that they were child sex tourists, a large number of whom intended to enter the country through Bali. Attempts to fly into Indonesia through Jakarta might have raised red flags if they did not look like businessmen, whereas it would have been easier to go through Denpasar immigration carrying tourist paraphernalia. Astonishingly, Indonesian officials told *The Sydney Morning Herald* that 92 of the hundreds barred were Australian child sex offenders.

Until 2014, Thailand, the Philippines and Malaysia were top of the list for visiting paedophiles, and then Indonesia, with its Bali jumping-off point, achieved the dubious number one position. In Australia many of those planning to fly to Bali didn't even get off the ground, with 20,000 on the National Child Offender Register having had their passports cancelled. But officials in Bali have made it known that there was every chance that paedophiles might have slipped through the immigration net.

Sydney's *Daily Telegraph* reported in August 2107 that foreigners were setting up orphanages in Bali under the guise of helping local children, while allegedly allowing paedophilia and sexual abuse by staff to occur. The paper quoted the former Victorian police officer, Glen Hulley – whose organisation Project Karma was behind the arrest of paedophile Robert Ellis – as saying that orphanages, some of which are illegitimate, are becoming a problem. His investigations had exposed foreigners and locals, mainly in remote areas of the island. The money offered to children in far-flung areas, he said, was a small fortune, resulting in the youngsters' abuse often being condoned by their parents.

So, there are the, gigolos, the prostitutes, the paedophiles and the ladyboys, all offering, or searching for, sex. A warning to all tourists walking along the beachfront at night comes in a wife's post on TripAdvisor in March 2013:

> We were walking home about 10 last night along the beach path near Motzzarella [restaurant] when two ladyboys grabbed both me and my husband and were pretending to dance with us. My one was trying to turn me away from my husband while his one was pretending to grab his crotch and steal his wallet. Luckily, I got free and hit the other one with my handbag so we got away but if someone was drunk it would be a different story. I wouldn't walk there at night and if you see the ladyboys keep well clear.

There were other similar stories: 'This actually happened to our neighbours late last year walking back to the Padma [resort in Legian]. They had their wallets and watches stolen and received some minor injuries.'

Another writer had also witnessed the 'dance with a ladyboy' tactic. 'Impossible to ignore them. They just grabbed us, initially acting as though it was fun i.e. the dancing but they had us by the wrists and wouldn't let go. They were on a bike so drove past us then stopped and got off, so we had to pass them. Hence why I felt the need for this post.'

Some social media posters say, however, that most ladyboys are good fun, but tourists have to be on their guard for an attempt at theft. One writer saw the amusing side of their choice of lifestyle: 'Yes, those ladyboys clearly need a good dressing down. Their dressing up is often less than convincing…Shame on them for muddying the reputation of [all] ladyboys.'

CHAPTER TWENTY-ONE

DOGS AND MONKEYS

Rain or shine, you'll see them running down Kuta Beach and splashing into the water. They'll shake themselves off and then jog along the water's edge as if on an important mission. Then they'll make their way back to the nearby lanes and streets looking for a spot of lunch. Tourists either love this particular band of locals – or hate them.

But one thing is certain, Bali dogs are a fascinating bunch, streetwise and then some, whether they're of the pure Kintamani breed which originated at the foot of a volcano in the island's north-east or whether they are street dogs which come from the other side of the tracks. They tend to tolerate one another as they run around Bali but they do have wide differences in backgrounds, appearances and a place they call home.

Many of the dogs that make their way to the beach daily are Kintamanis that have owners who let them out to roam and play, knowing that at the end of the day, or earlier, they'll head back home for food. Whereas the common street dog won't have a home to go to and will have to forage for whatever food it can find. It will sleep in the middle of the road after dark in quiet villages, getting up from time to time to howl and bark. That I can testify to, almost running over one while driving at two o'clock in the morning after a late evening with a group of Balinese friends.

The Kintamani is that white furred dog you see frolicking on the beach, usually ignoring the calls of 'Here boy!' from animal loving tourists or the 'Get away!' yells of others who fear they are going to be attacked and catch rabies. The dogs will protect themselves if they feel threatened, giving a warning snarl or even a bite if someone tries to kick them away. I've seen it happen with a large German man who threw a bare foot towards one of the animals, only to receive a nip on the ankle.

The Balinese people themselves take no notice of the dogs that come foraging, although they will shoo them away from the front of restaurants if tourists start to object to their presence.

Various theories have been put forward to explain where the Kintamani breed originated, but it gets its name from the Kintamani region, a picturesque part of the island about an hour's drive from Ubud. The area is marked by Mount Batur, remarkable due to the fact that a temple sits on the rim of the active volcano.

In mid-August 2017 dogs of all breeds living in villages in the shadow of the huge Mount Agung volcano, in east Bali, pricked up their ears. Some began to growl while others moved around restlessly. Village elders recognised the warning signs – the volcano was waking.

There were no other indications that the volcano was posing a threat but the unusual behaviour of the dogs and other farm animals was watched carefully by villagers 'in the know'. They warned families to be ready to move. Then in late August officials said they had detected shallow tremors on their monitoring equipment. As the days went by Mount Agung began to show increasing signs of activity and it was decided to begin evacuations of villages surrounding the volcano.

By mid-September some 40,000 people had been evacuated amid hundreds of tremors and signs of magma rising to the rim of the volcano. A 12-kilometre exclusion zone was imposed around the mountain and by early October all the warnings remained in place as displaced families wondered when they would be able to return to their homes. Officials warned them it could be a long wait.

Highly intelligent, fun and unique, Kintamani dogs are to be found everywhere in the mountain region and even though most have owners, they will find a place to build a kind of nest to give birth to their young and they'll also find comfort in a cave. Just how they got to the area is credited to a Chinese trader called Lee who landed at Singaraja on the north coast, sometime between the twelfth and sixteenth centuries, coming ashore with his chow chow dog. The trader, his family and the dog made their way to the Mount Batur region where they settled and the chow chow got to make its own friends with the local feral girl dogs. Soon dogs that were a cross between chow chows and the ferals started populating the area and the Kintamani dog was, in the centuries that followed, to become a unique breed. Historians trying to establish if Mr Lee and his chow chow were responsible were convinced that he had indeed lived in the shadow of

Mount Batur because a Chinese temple had been found in the area; an icon at which people of the Confucian faith still pray today.

There is, however, another, and perhaps less convincing theory, about the lineage of the Kintamani dog. While it is generally accepted that the animal evolved from Balinese feral dogs, which in turn are linked to Asian canines such as the Australian dingo, it has been suggested that the breed was brought to Bali by invaders from the Javanese kingdom of Majapahit in the mid-1300s. Another theory has the dog coming to Bali with Javanese refugees of the fifteenth century civil war. However, Mr Lee and his dog appear to be the originators of the Kintamanis so loved or despised by tourists.

The mixed-breed feral dogs have owners too, despite the suggestion that they might be 'wild'. The ownership is rather different to Western styles, for they are comfortable sleeping on doorsteps or in courtyards, because they have formed a bond with the people who live there and the Balinese believe having a dog around helps to keep intruders at bay.

But it's not all hunky dory for a dog in Bali. It's said that back in 2008 the dog population on the island was about 600,000 and then came a rabies outbreak, resulting in government death squads gunning down strays in a mass culling programme. That reduced the numbers to around 150,000, resulting in animal lovers warning that if the shootings and poisonings continued the world-famous Bali dogs, made up of 'commoners' and Kintamanis, would die out. There was – and remains – added pressure on the dog population with reportedly hundreds of them dying each week to the dog meat trade, disease, motor vehicle accidents and neglect.

Unthinkable to the Western world, some Balinese, and Indonesians all around the Republic, are not averse to eating dog meat.

I was once invited to a barbecue by a local friend in Bali and jokingly asked if he was going to serve me dog meat. 'But yes, of course, it's the best,' he said. 'It will be very fresh.' Naturally, I declined, his comments about 'very fresh' suggesting to me that an animal might have been killed for the barbecue. Eating dog meat is not illegal in Indonesia, with many locals believing it can even be beneficial to health.

My experience was not unique – and please note, if you are disturbed about animal cruelty, skip the next couple of paragraphs.

In June 2017, the ABC, following a special investigation, reported that tourists were unknowingly being fed dog meat during their Bali vacations. The broadcaster claimed that dogs were being grabbed off the streets, brutally butchered and then sold as grilled, barbecued or sautéed, meat to unsuspecting tourists at street kiosks and some restaurants. An investigator for the ABC found that thousands of dogs were being bludgeoned to death, hung, poisoned or shot. One dog catcher claimed he alone had killed thousands of dogs – 12 a week. A street vendor in Seminyak admitted that what he was selling was 'dog satay'. But cooks will mostly deny it to those tourists who ask whether the meat is dog, so they go ahead and order, without realising that's just what the food is. Even respectable-looking restaurants will sell satay or 'steak with vegetables', which is dog meat. Health specialists in the Western world are alarmed, believing there are serious health risks with eating canine meat because there's a chance the animal might have been killed with poison.

Dr Andrew Dawson, director of the New South Wales Poisons Information Centre told the ABC that if a dog had died from cyanide the poison, the poison was not going to be destroyed by cooking. A curry which included pieces of the animal's stomach or heart would carry high concentrations of cyanide, which could be fatal.

Tourists who crave meat can usually avoid eating dog flesh by checking if the letters RW are posted on the outside of a restaurant. They stand for the Indonesian words rintek wuuk, which is literally translated to mean 'soft fur', which translated further means 'dog meat'.

Meanwhile, the Kintamani breed and their more lowly cousins continue to splash at the water's edge in Kuta and Legian and the tourists snap away with their cameras. The dogs are a hit on social media. And if they're the lucky ones, they'll get to live out their days until, for them, the famous sunset finally fades away.

• • •

There's a different kind of animal movement in the higher ground far above Kuta. The trees rustle, the air is shattered by screeches. The monkeys of Ubud are at play. Their playthings are the humans that pop into their world.

I've been to the Bali Monkey Forest and know that the complaints by terrified tourists about muggings, theft and aggression are true, having been tugged and pulled in all directions by a screeching gang that suspected I was carrying fruit. I guessed they could smell the fruit I'd had on my breakfast muesli. But perhaps I'll leave it to Amy who wrote a blog (Our Big Fat Travel Adventure) about the experience she and her companion Andrew had in the forest.

'Before we even arrived we started hearing horror stories about the Monkey Forest; animals stealing cameras and wallets, chasing people and worse still, biting. A bite can be extremely painful at the best of times, but in Bali there's another hazard to consider – rabies.'

She and Andrew had taken the precaution before they left England to have pre-rabies vaccinations and they also ensured that all they would take with them to the forest would be a camera. They might have felt safe, but then a small monkey, playing in a puddle after a torrential rainstorm, suddenly turned on Amy's companion, leaping onto his shoulder, nipping around his neck and working his way down to his waist.

'With seasoned ease he promptly shoved his skinny, thieving hand deep into Andrew's pocket, rummaging around for treasurers. Horror-struck, I watched as the monkey turned his attention to our camera case which, although firmly closed, was soon unzipped by the little pickpocket, who grabbed a lens cap and hopped down.'

They managed to retrieve the lens cap but the couple admitted they were feeling uncomfortable at this point, particularly after they saw another monkey bite a visitor on his arm. Pressure from the monkeys became so intense that Amy and her companion decided to get out of the forest enclosure, 'yes, we were literally chased out of the Monkey Forest, but at least we escaped unscathed.' Amy's advice: 'if you're heading to the Ubud Monkey Forest, please be careful not to take anything with you. Cover up and wear closed shoes as the animals are likely to jump on you. Don't bring food or try to touch the monkeys. Respect them for the wild animals they are.'

While unsuspecting tourists described fearful experiences in the Sacred Monkey Forest Sanctuary, residents of the nearby village of Padangtegal, who actually own the land, regard it as an important spiritual, economic, educational and conservation centre for their village. Their reference to 'education' encompasses the fact that the habits of the 700 or so monkeys that live in the forest can be a learning experience. And in those 12.5 hectares there are more than 186 species of trees.

The keepers are well aware of the fear that some visitors have as they step through the forest gate. It is right there, at the entrance, that it is suggested that plastic or paper bags and plastic bottles should be entrusted to the ticket office. The monkeys, say the villagers, will generally not approach people if they don't bring bananas or other food with them. Anyone who does want to feed a banana to a monkey should do it carefully, and never try to pull it back because an ugly fight is certain to follow.

There are parts of the forest that are prohibited to tourists because they are regarded as sacred. And anyone who wants to visit a temple area can only do so if they intend to pray and wear proper Balinese praying dress.

The monkeys of Bali have been around since the beginning of time – or at least for as long as Indonesia was one huge chunk of land and mankind was graduating from ape to human. The animals that live on the Island of Gods are officially known as *Macaca fascicularis* – long-tailed macaque. And like modern man, they have their families and cousins and their conflicts with others over land. They even have babysitters; a female that is not a parent will often look after a baby to help the mother out.

While the Monkey Forest in Ubud is the main attraction for overseas visitors, macaque monkeys can be found in many others parts of Bali, mostly around temples, the carved stone of which provided plenty of 'sitting and watching' places. It's estimated there are around 63 temple sites over-run by several hundred monkeys.

Professor Bruce Wheatley of the University of Alabama, in a comprehensive study of the macaque and its cultural and historical basis, points out that the animals enjoy a prominent and even sacred standing in Balinese culture and religion. 'Their prominence emanates in large part from the role played by monkeys in the Ramayana, a Hindu epic poem that is particularly popular among Balinese Hindus,' he says.

According to Professor Wheatley, monkeys associated with Hindu temples are often tolerated and even treated with kindness in Balinese society. They appear to occupy a border area between the animal and demonic world and the world of humans – alternatively, between the world of humans and the world of gods. As such, the Balinese consider, the monkey has the power to move between worlds.

They can also move between groups of tourists in the Monkey Forest, generating great enjoyment with a collection of cute photographs – to post on Instagram or Facebook – or abject fear.

There's no doubt that they are exceptionally intelligent – and cunning. The respected *New Scientist* even suggested that at one location, the Uluwatu Temple, a stunning place of Hindu prayer perched on the edge of a cliff in south Bali, a monkey mafia presides. There, the animals steal tourists' belongings, only returning them in exchange for food, bartering over everything from hats, to glasses, to wads of cash.

Their behaviour, however, is important from a scientific angle. Researchers from Belgium's University of Liege suggest that since the Uluwatu Temple is the only place where monkeys run a food-for-goods exchange service, their behaviour must be observed. Scientists say that the animals have learned today's tricks from previous generations. Getting information about the behaviour of this particular group of bandits at Uluwatu was not easy, primatologist Fany Brotcorne told *New Scientist*. 'The monkeys were always trying to steal my hat, my pen, even my research data.'

Back at the Ubud Monkey Forest, keepers insist that none of the animals have rabies as they are tested for the potentially fatal disease annually. But Anthony Wallace, a New South Wales man wasn't taking any chances after a monkey jumped onto his shoulders and bit him deeply on his bald head. He was told by a doctor that if he got rabies, he would die. This spurred him into undergoing treatment, which included four immunoglobulin injections into his scalp, resulting in his head 'puffing up like a balloon'. He also had to undergo four shots of rabies vaccine over a period of two weeks. 'It's not something you'd like to see others go through,' he said.

So, whether it's as dog or a monkey that inflicts a bite, it's natural for the receiver to be concerned about contracting a disease, the worst being rabies. While the chances of being infected are slim, the risk is there and remains part of the Indonesian government's health concerns, particularly as seven new cases emerged in the Regency of Tabanan, in central Bali, in January 2017. *The Bali Post* reported that one resident suffered rabies, followed shortly after in another part of the regency, when six people went down with the disease.

The six who needed treatment were bitten by a tiny Kintamani puppy which had been purchased in late December at a local market. Over a two-week period, the two-month-old dog had been played with, despite it displaying aggressive behaviour and biting anyone who approached it. The owner reported the bites to health officials and it was decided to put the dog down. A sample of brain matter confirmed the dog was infected with rabies. Health authorities, determined to prevent the spread of rabies in all areas of the island, urged dog owners not to travel with their pets outside their home environment unless the animals had been vaccinated against rabies.

Fishermen travelling with their dogs from other islands were suspected of being the cause of a rabies outbreak in Uluwatu in 2008, which then spread to Denpasar and other parts. Until then Bali had been free of rabies for over ten years. At the Sanglah hospital, the rabies clinic was under pressure to treat some 1000 bites a month, resulting in a severe shortage of rabies vaccine. In one sad case two young boys who were given the vaccine after they were bitten still died because the second drug that was required, immunoglobulin, was unavailable.

During 2015, 15 people died in Bali from rabies while in the previous two years there had been only three deaths. The increase in numbers spread panic among the authorities, who were convinced that something had to be done to stop the spread. So, onto the streets went the shooters with strychnine-laced darts. Piles of dogs were loaded onto trucks and burned. It was a grim sight, but it saved the dogs from a lingering death and helped to cut down the numbers of humans who were bitten by rabid animals.

A midwife and nurse who has been living in Bali for more than 30 years, has drawn up a list of the warning signs. Kim Patra says the first symptoms of rabies are similar to flu, with a fever, headache and fatigue. This is followed by respiratory, gastrointestinal and/or central nervous system problems. Rabies in its critical stage brings hyperactivity or paralysis. The victim falls into a coma and, without intensive care, death follows within seven days, usually due to breathing failure.

• • •

It's not just dog bites that can afflict visitors. In a tragic case, a mother and daughter died in Bali just 24 hours after arriving there for a holiday in January 2014. A coroner in Queensland found that Noelene Bischoff aged 54, and her 14-year-old daughter Yvana, from Queensland's Sunshine Coast, died from an allergic reaction to food, likely to have been fish. Asthma was a contributing factor, along with, in the mother's case, obesity, coroner Terry Ryan found.

Mother and daughter had died within hours of one another after eating fish at the Padang Bay Beach Resort on the east coast of the island at the start of their 15-day holiday, Noelene dying in an ambulance and her daughter passing away in hospital. The management strongly denied that food poisoning was the cause of death. Nolene and Yvana were brought back to Australia and buried together in the Lockyer Valley, west of Brisbane.

In March 2017 came reports of another Australian woman dying in Bali, but this time police said 38-year-old Summa Simmonds's death was due to allegedly consuming more than a bottle of vodka at the luxury Peppers Seminyak resort. In addition to drinking the bottle of vodka, said police, she had also consumed six more shots in the evening.

'When she went to her villa, she began vomiting,' said Badung Police Precinct Chief Budi Setiawan. 'She fainted, was unconscious and her pulse became weak. The victim's face and lips turned blue.'

Ms Simmonds's sister and a friend performed CPR and asked reception staff to call urgently for a doctor. But the doctor was unable to save her. One friend wrote on social media, 'I'm so numb. I can't believe that a beautiful soul has been taken away so soon.' Ms Simmonds's family and friends disputed that she drank as much as the police claimed, and suggested she had died from a reaction to the alcohol.

But the sad case involving Noelene and her daughter and that of Summa are extremes. Overseas visitors come and go by the millions each year and return home with fond memories. But some don't make it home, however. Not just because of death by natural causes, by accidents, allergic reactions, road crashes, drownings or because of contracting a fatal disease – but because they have ended up behind bars, facing a bleak future.

CHAPTER TWENTY-TWO

THE BALI NINE

On the evening of Sunday, 17 April 2005, Bali's Ngurah Rai Airport was crowded, as usual, with homeward-bound tourists. Many were due to fly towards South-East Asia and onwards to Europe, while some were headed east. But the majority were Australians with destinations in Brisbane, Sydney, Melbourne and Perth. They were suntanned, laughing, as they remembered a particular fun moment or joking as they wondered whether they should try for an upgrade.

Bags were packed with souvenirs, wooden idols, hats, T-shirts, folded-up kites. Children with hair coloured and braided waited patiently as their parents moved slowly down the check-in queue. Surfers, with hair turned blonde by the sun and the sea waited with their girlfriends. Honeymoon couples held hands. For the airline staff it was just an ordinary night. Tomorrow it would be repeated, different people, same scenes.

But it wasn't quite ordinary: four of the passengers on this particular night were carrying extra baggage which they had no intention of declaring. Scott Rush, 19, Michael Czugaj, also 19, Renae Lawrence, 27, and Martin Stephens, 29, had drugs wrapped in plastic and strapped to their legs or bodies — a total of 8.3 kilograms of heroin worth $4 million at the time. There was nothing about their shapes that disclosed the hidden narcotics, but there was no way they were going to be allowed to board their plane.

What the four did not know was that every move they had made, not just that evening at the airport, but in the days leading up to their arrival there, had been monitored by undercover police. One man associated with the four, Andrew Chan, 21, did make it onto his flight, Australian Airlines flight 7830 bound for Australia, but he was arrested and taken off the plane before it left the departure gate.

As for the four who were still waiting to board, police moved in on them and took them to a private room where they were ordered to strip. There were no excuses; could be no excuses. Collectively, they were carrying a commercial quantity of drugs. Whether one had more than the other did not matter. They were in it together. As far as Bali's narcotics police were concerned the arrests were guaranteed a long time earlier.

But there were others to be rounded up. Police swooped on the Melasti Hotel in beachside Legian and arrested four other members of the smuggling gang: Myuran Sukumaran, 24, Tan Duc Thanh Nguyen, 27, Si Yi Chen, 20, and Matthew Norman, 18. All together eight men and one woman were placed under arrest, resulting in media around the world referring to them as the Bali Nine.

Why had they been such an easy catch? Nine members of a drug gang being pulled in at three different places at the same time – on a plane, at the airport, in a hotel – suggested top police work. As events were to develop it became clear that Balinese narcotics officers had received a sound tip-off and all they had to do was wait until that Sunday evening in April 2005 to swoop. The smugglers were lambs to the slaughter.

As news spread about the dramatic arrests, one chilling fact emerged. Anyone convicted of dealing with such a large quantity of narcotics – Bali's biggest heroin bust – faced execution under Indonesia's tough anti-narcotics laws.

During initial inquiries, it was to be claimed, Renae Lawrence was heard telling the others who had been arrested at the airport, 'By dobbing some other **** I'm not killing my family. And what's the point, anyway, because if we dob them in, right, we dob them in. They'll kill our family and then we're dead anyway. So, you know why…don't tell them and they'll just kill us instead and leave our families alone.'

The Bali Nine were made up of two groups, from Melbourne and Sydney, and one link to them all appeared to be a multinational catering company with thousands of employees. Renae Lawrence, Martin Stephens, Matthew Norman and Andrew Chan worked for the company, which had impressive clients, including the Sydney Cricket Club. And while it is thought the smuggling plan was discussed while that group were working together, Scott Rush and Michael Czugaj allegedly admitted they were recruited into the smuggling plan by Tan Duc Thanh Nguyen, said to be the plot's financier, while they were socialising at a karaoke bar in Brisbane.

Norman, it was later established, had met Nguyen six months before their arrests while fishing. They had then travelled to Melbourne together where Rush was introduced to Sukumaran. During 'friendly chats' Nguyen asked the other two if they'd like an all-expenses-paid trip to Bali. It was an offer they couldn't refuse, but as it turned out, there were strings attached.

Scott Rush's father, Lee, was alarmed when his son told him he was going to Bali on a free trip. Nothing in this life is that free, thought Lee, and he smelled trouble. He knew his son had used drugs in the past and he feared narcotics were involved in the planned trip to Bali. Scott had started out using marijuana, followed by ecstasy and heroin and had been expelled from a Brisbane college for drug use. In 2004 he'd pleaded guilty in a magistrates court to drug possession, drink-driving, theft and fraud.

His father decided that something had to be done to prevent Scott going to Bali, so he contacted a lawyer friend. Between them it was agreed that Scott had to be stopped somehow and the idea emerged to contact the Australian Federal Police (AFP) and get them to block Scott from leaving the country on the grounds he was planning something illegal. Yes, police allegedly assured the worried father, Scott would be stopped.

But it didn't work out that way. Nothing was done to prevent the flight. In fact police, deciding that Scott was an adult and there was no evidence that he had up to that point done anything wrong, tipped off Indonesian National Police about the possibility of a crime in the making. In fact, Australian narcotics officials had strong grounds for believing this because they had been watching Nguyen for several months. The Vietnamese-Australian and others had travelled to Bali on an earlier occasion to organise the export of heroin to Australia but the plan was abandoned because not enough money could be raised to purchase the drug. Now Nguyen was ready to try again and Scott Rush would be one of the mules.

On tipping off the Indonesians, Australian police were assured that Rush, Nguyen and all those they associated with in Bali, would be placed under strict scrutiny. Lee Rush's fears about his son's determination to fly to Bali were confirmed when a travel agent phoned the Rush home on 7 April 7 2005, to confirm Scott's booking to fly to Denpasar the following day.

'This phone call made us feel absolutely sick in the stomach,' Lee Rush told the ABC in 2006. 'It was a gut feeling more than anything. Possibly there was some link with drugs.'

Despite no attempt being made to stop Scott Rush from leaving Australia, on the same day the teenager left, 8 April 2005, the AFP sent a letter to their Indonesian counterparts, headed 'Subject: Heroin couriers from Bali to Australia'.

Other members of the smuggling gang had already left Australia, but all would be scheduled to leave a week later with the heroin hidden under loose-fitting clothing. Their instructions were to avoid carrying or wearing anything metal which would set off detectors at the airport. And they should bring with them wooden carvings that they would declare to quarantine officials in Australia, which would enable them to be waved through customs without further searches.

In the AFP alert to the Indonesians, Bali police were asked to not only keep the group under surveillance, but to try to establish who was supplying the drugs. Whatever evidence was gained, said the AFP, would enable Australian authorities to arrest the group on their return. But the AFP created a loophole for the Indonesians, stating in their correspondence that if Bali officers suspected 'that Chan and/or the couriers are in possession of drugs at the time of their departure, that they take what action they deem appropriate.'

It was highly unlikely that the Indonesians were going to turn their backs on such a big catch and allow the Australians to fly home, for any arrests and the subsequent publicity would spread the message that the Republic did not and would not tolerate drugs. Local officers were given a further incentive to catch the group on their territory when, four days after the initial brief, the AFP informed the Balinese of dates, times and flight details of the smugglers' return to Australia.

Just why the AFP had left it open for Balinese authorities to arrest the group was unclear but it might have been an attempt to win support with the Indonesians in relation to counterterrorism operations. In any case, the actions of the AFP, which placed nine Australians at risk of being executed, raised the anger of the New South Wales Council for Civil Liberties, which described the behaviour of the federal body as outrageous.

Several members of the group had a history of problems. Aside from Rush and his drug background in Australia, Renae Lawrence, from Newcastle, north of Sydney, came from a broken home. In her teenage years and into her twenties she lived in a same-sex relationship with a mother of three children who was ten years older. When it ended, Lawrence moved back in with her mother and stepfather. Her father, Bob Lawrence, told Australian media that she was naive and 'bloody stupid'. She was not a bad kid, he said, she just happened to get in with the wrong mob. She was doing it tough, never had much money.

Lawrence worked at first with a car smash-repair firm, before later getting a job with the same catering company where Andrew Chan, Martin Stephens and Matthew Norman worked. Lawrence and Norman had a problem some three weeks before they flew to Bali when they were driving along the Pacific Highway in a stolen vehicle and were stopped by police using road spikes and arrested. They were due to appear in court in Gosford, north of Sydney, on 26 April 2005, but by then they were both behind bars in Bali, awaiting a trial that could result in them being sentenced to death.

Renae Lawrence's incarceration in Bali brought to an end a very dangerous game she had been playing. Investigations following her arrest at the airport revealed that six months earlier, in October 2004, she had been invited to Andrew Chan's home to celebrate her twenty-seventh birthday, and it was there that Chan allegedly asked her to travel to Bali with him, with all expenses paid. While she was to claim later that she was not told why she was being invited on the trip, Chan had told her that she would be rewarded if she followed his instructions, but if she disclosed the nature of their soon-to-be-revealed arrangement there would be problems for her family.

In that month of October, she flew to Bali on a dummy run and on what Indonesian police said was a false passport, although she was to deny that accusation. Chan arrived on the island on the same date. Then the two of them met Sukumaran, who strapped packages to the bodies of Lawrence and Chan, then, accompanied by Chan's girlfriend, Grace, the two flew back to Australia. Incredibly, they cleared customs and immigration both in Bali and Australia. Back home, she was to reveal, she received an envelope containing $10,000. Her money troubles were over for the time being.

She tried it again, under Chan's instructions in December, although she was to claim that seven others were involved. But the operation, involving heroin, had to be abandoned because the suppliers feared that details had leaked out. On 6 April, however, Lawrence was paid cash while Stephens, who was to fly with her, was threatened if he didn't go. The plan was to fly back to Australia with heroin on 14 April, but Chan became worried that police in Australia and Indonesia had learned about the smuggling operation. The date was set for 17 April; and that was the date that proved to be both disastrous and potentially fatal.

Like Lawrence, Scott Rush was facing charges in Australia when he was arrested in Bali. A warrant had been issued against him in relation to the theft of $4,796.95 from a bank. He and his friend Michael Czugaj had met Tan Duc Thanh Nguyen in a hotel in Brisbane's Fortitude Valley, a glitzy nightclub area close to the city centre. Rush was to claim that his and Czugaj's Bali downfall was the result of them being offered a free holiday on the island by Nguyen. When the two teenagers checked into the Hotel Aneka they had no inkling that it was under surveillance by Indonesian police.

Wandering around Bali, they went by arrangement to the Hard Rock Hotel, right on the Kuta beachfront, where Nguyen introduced them to Andrew Chan and Myuran Sukumaran. It was then, the teenagers were to claim, Chan and Sukumaran threatened that if they refused to hide packages on their body when they returned home their families would be killed.

As with Lawrence and Rush, Czugaj did not have an unblemished background, his parents describing him as a 'problem child'. He had a background of small-time crime which included evading paying for train fares, wilful damage, receiving stolen property and drink driving. Even so, one of eight children born to his Polish-Australian parents, he had a steady job as an apprentice glazier, and spent many enjoyable hours surfing in Queensland. His parents were stunned when he told them he was leaving his job and going to Cairns for a holiday.

Yet another player in the Bali drugs plot, Andrew Chan, had a dark background. He was the youngest child of Chinese migrants and while his parents appeared to do well running restaurants, at school in Sydney their son was considered a trickster and a bully. He also started taking drugs when he got the job with the catering company. His own use of drugs moved him into narcotics smuggling.

He was to tell SBS TV's *Dateline* programme later:

> I don't think I was going anywhere in life. I don't think, you know, I was achieving too much, even though I had a stable job and all…I've used drugs myself. I was a drug user. You know, I know what it feels like to, to be, you know, one of them junkies walking on the street. You don't think too much about – I didn't anyway.

Myuran Sukumaran also had a flawed history. London born to Sri Lankan parents, he moved with his family to Australia when he was four years old. He was on the receiving end of racism and bullying at school in south-west Sydney and later dropped out of university. His jobs as a mailroom clerk and then in the Sydney passport office struck him as being too mundane and he wanted more. He began using drugs and entered an alternative world of nightclubs and fast cars, evolving into drug pushing after he fell into the criminal world.

Matthew Norman, the youngest member of the Bali Nine, was also not blemish free. It was he who was arrested in March 2005 with Renae Lawrence as they sped along the Pacific Highway in a stolen car, police finally stopping them by bursting the tyres with road spikes.

Si Yi Chen was 12 when his family brought him from China to Australia, but he was to hint at early problems when he said, with a touch of a Chinese accent, that he was the 'luckiest kid…because we always get away with troubles when we were young.' His parents were strict, too strict, so he rebelled about being denied the chance to go to places of entertainment like the movies with his schoolmates. His parents made him stay at home to study, but when an argument with his father ensued over his decision not to go to university he moved out of the family home.

Did he move into selling drugs? 'I started living by myself and then, of course, you need money to survive,' he said, suggesting that is just what he did.

Vietnamese-Australian Tan Duc Thanh Nguyen, was described as the 'forgotten Bali Nine member', mainly because he was moved around in prisons in Indonesia and so was not the centre of publicity. Nguyen had a dubious background. He had been identified as the financial recruiter for the heroin-smuggling plot and had arranged the earlier smuggling attempt that had to be aborted. There was no doubt he had access to funds because he was able to pay for the flights to Bali by other members of the Bali Nine. However, he was to deny that he had money to spare because in Australia he had supported his four younger sisters, paying for their education.

So, the heroin was grabbed by Bali police. But the immediate question, posed by both the AFP and Indonesian authorities, was: who supplied it?

The chief suspect, but certainly not the mastermind, was a 22-year-old Thai prostitute, using her working name of 'Cherry' Likit Bannakorn. With no obvious source for such a large amount of heroin in Bali, it is believed she herself was a drug mule, risking death if caught smuggling it into the island from Bangkok. Having delivered the heroin, she is thought to have left Bali on 18 April, checking out of the Seaview Hotel, Kuta, the day after the Australians were arrested, perhaps flying to the Malaysian capital, Kuala Lumpur. She was later detained at the land border between Malaysia and Thailand. Hot on her tail, Indonesian police, by arrangement with Thai police, arrived at the border with the intention of taking her back to Bali. But they hit a snag. The paperwork to detain this crucial link in the plot did not qualify her to be extradited to Indonesia. The authorities had to let her go. Not surprisingly, Cherry vanished and is today on Interpol's wanted list.

Her 'escape' was a big miss, for it transpired that she had allegedly made several drug runs in the South-East Asian region. Experienced in the ways of avoiding detection, she might have been able to provide names of others involved in the Bali operation and other plots.

Provided with samples of the heroin found on the Australians, AFP scientists established that the heroin had originated in Myanmar (Burma), most likely being produced in the Golden Triangle, which straddles Myanmar, Thailand, Laos and China. Police believe the drugs went from Myanmar into Thailand, and from Bangkok Cherry took them to Bali.

The AFP Commissioner at the time, Mick Keelty, told the ABC that Cherry, 'a person of interest', was 'a Thai national and the fact that we believe that the transiting of the drugs was most likely through Thailand, she does become an important player.'

One other suspected link to the smuggling chain, Nepalese-born Man Singh Ghale, was shot dead in Jakarta by Indonesian police during an alleged escape attempt a few days after the arrest of the Bali Nine. But the AFP said later he was not the Mr Big of the operation and there were questions about the nature of his death because he was handcuffed at the time and any escape attempt would have been futile.

There were continued questions, too, about the decision by the AFP to tip off the Indonesians about the suspected planned drug run. 'I know it's an emotive issue…but we can't apologise for taking the strategy forward,' Commissioner Mick Keelty said on Southern Cross Broadcasting. 'While we have some sympathy for the potential outcome [a reference to possible death sentences], we've got to be looking at the bigger picture all the time.'

He repeated that it was the call of the Indonesian police on whether the Australians were arrested in Bali or whether they should be allowed to fly back to Australia to be picked up. In a letter to the Indonesians in which Jakarta was tipped-off, said Mr Keelty, it was specified that the AFP was trying to identify the entire syndicate.

As for the whereabouts of Cherry, she had totally disappeared.

CHAPTER TWENTY-THREE

THEY SANG HYMNS BEFORE THE RIFLES BLAZED

Did Cherry survive? Was anyone ever really going to let her loose? Is she still running drugs to this day? Has she forsaken the risk-taking, changed her name, slipped back into the seedy world or prostitution? Married? Become a mother?

Also known by the alias of Pina, I do wonder if the woman who, without her flashy make-up looks very plain in an old black-and-white police mugshot, is alive today. She was being used because she was expendable.

A prostitute being hunted by the world's police through Interpol, who was also being targeted by her drug-running masters…she had little to no chance of remaining on the loose. If the police had found her, it is most likely we would have heard about her arrest by now – unless she was placed in protective custody and given a totally new identity in exchange for telling all that she knew.

She had spoken briefly to Thai police, but they wanted more – much more – and it wasn't forthcoming.

After her narrow escape on the Malaysian-Thai border, drug bosses would regard Cherry as a danger to their operation. No matter how adept she might have been in the past, smuggling drugs through airports or border checkpoints, she had slipped up this time. She'd failed to close down her trail back to Thailand and that was a bad mistake. Drug kings don't like mistakes. It's possible that decisions were made to silence Cherry Likit Bannakorn; under narcotic officers' brutal interrogation there was little doubt she would reveal all in exchange for being treated leniently.

Little is known about Cherry's background, but it is believed that like many young women selling sex in the bars of Bangkok she had made her way from an outlying town, such as those close to the border with Laos, seeking a quick and easy way to make money to send back to her poverty-stricken family. From prostitution it was a mere sidestep to enter the drug world. She moved into an apartment block in Bangkok, where witnesses claimed to have seen her in the company of a number of Nigerian men. Whether they were involved in the drug ring which sent Cherry off to various South-East Asian countries is not known, but it's clear that someone was giving her very clear instructions.

It is also not known how Cherry initially communicated with Andrew Chan, but it can be safely assumed that her rendezvous with Chan in room 114 of the Sea View Hotel, when she delivered a suitcase to him, was arranged by drug kingpins.

It is unclear whether Cherry was actually trying to re-enter Thailand through Malaysia when she was caught on the border or whether she was on her way out of her home country, but in any case, she was searched, and no drugs were found on her. During her temporary detention, however, Cherry gave police a few details about her travels.

According to Police Commissioner Watcharapon Prasenrachakit, the head of Thailand's Narcotics Suppression Bureau, Cherry admitted she had made two journeys to Bali in 2005, the most recent being in April 2005 – a reference, presumably, to the trip that resulted in the arrest of the Bali Nine. In an interview with the Australian Broadcasting Corporation, Mr Watcharapon outlined the few details police had established about her movements.

'We found out she travelled from Bangkok to Phuket and from Phuket she flew with Silk Air to Singapore and from there we don't have any information. We don't know how she happened to be in Bali at the time that there was an arrest on the Australian group.'

Added to the confusion as to exactly how Cherry came to hook up with Andrew Chan, the narcotics chief said she had met him at a nightclub in Bali, not, as Chan had said, in the Sea View Hotel. 'Mr Chan is one of her maybe temporary boyfriends, something like that,' said Mr Watcharapon.

According to the police officer Cherry claimed Chan had paid for sex and that she had not met him previously. In Bangkok, he said, she had stayed in various places while working as a call girl, but had also been able to provide eight separate 'short-time hotels' where prostitutes take their clients.

'Sex workers are frequently used by drug bosses to carry narcotics,' said the officer. And in one astonishing revelation, without revealing – or being able to – who was behind her travel arrangements, Cherry admitted she had been to Columbia, the cocaine capital of the world.

Police, anxious to establish who was behind her movements but failing to obtain names, addresses or phone numbers, were able to follow Cherry's recent movements through immigration records, and what they found astonished them. The young prostitute had successfully travelled with heroin down through Thailand to the Malaysian border. From Malaysia she had flown to Jakarta and then on to South Africa. On one trip she had apparently travelled empty handed to Columbia, before flying out of the country with cocaine, using the same route. Cherry's bank account showed frequent payments of $1000, a large sum for a poor girl from rural Thailand.

Why use someone like Cherry, trusting her with a fortune in narcotics? Police suspect it's simply because she looks so 'innocent' that customs officials barely give her a second glance.

On the way back to Thailand, said Commissioner Watcharapon, couriers like Cherry would travel by car across the border from Malaysia. She had done it enough times to feel confident that she wouldn't be stopped with drugs in her possession.

'We found that this syndicate, normally in war with the West African syndicate, will use a Thai bar girl of very low education and they don't have enough money. So, they've been victimised by this syndicate to carry out drugs (heroin) and carry in cocaine.'

On her arrival back in Thailand after her detention – and then freedom due to a problem with her extradition to Indonesia – Cherry was allowed to continue on to one of the many residences she was using. But she ended up on Interpol's wanted list, and that made her a number-one target for both Thai officials and the stop-at-nothing drug syndicates who knew that her information presented a danger to them.

As police and narcotics officers were trying to establish more details of Cherry's involvement in the heroin smuggling operation, two members of the Bali Nine were preparing to become the first of the group to go before a court in Bali – and their roles were in stark contrast. At 19 years of age, Michael Czugaj from Brisbane, being the youngest, was regarded as being at the bottom end of the scale while 24-year-old Myuran Sukumaran, from

Sydney, was seen as one of the kingpins, along with Andrew Chan. The teenager and Sukumaran – referred to in reports as the babe and the beast – had been warned that prosecutors were going to seek the death penalty, but their lawyers, and legal representatives for the entire nine, said they would ask the court to consider charges of drug possession, rather than trafficking, which would impose a maximum jail sentence of ten years.

Czugaj, looking younger than his 19 years and wearing a white shirt and a baseball cap, was led into a separate courtroom on 11 October 2005, while Sukumaran, a burly figure with a shaved head, was hustled before judges some 40 metres away in the sprawling court complex. Czugaj's mother Vicki was in court, watching her son playing with a keychain containing an image of the Virgin Mary.

Sukumaran, said the prosecution in the nearby court, had helped to recruit Czugaj in Brisbane, and it was also Sukumaran who had helped tape the drug packages to the four 'mules' arrested at the airport, Czugaj, Renae Lawrence, Martin Stephens and Scott Rush. During the opening of the two men's trials, the name of Andrew Chan was mentioned by Sukumaran's prosecutor, Olopan Nainggolan, who said Chan had arranged the initial meetings in Sydney when the drug run was plotted. Chan had also booked the airline tickets and hotels. Chan, too, had received a black suitcase containing the heroin from Cherry, when they met in the Sea View Hotel on 15 April.

The prosecution said that under the plan, Sukumaran had told Czugaj, Lawrence, Rush and Stephens that when they arrived back in Australia with the heroin they were to get in touch with a person known to Sukumaran as 'Pinocchio'. The court heard just how much each 'mule' was carrying: Czugaj 1.75 kilograms, Rush 1.69 kilograms, Lawrence 2.16 kilograms and Stephens 2.34 kilograms. Another amount of heroin, 334 grams, along with scissors and tape, was found with Sukumaran and others in the second group – Nguyen, Chen and Norman – at the Melasti Beach Hotel. In Czugaj's courtroom, prosecutors outlined the same background. There was no sign that any leniency was going to be granted to either man.

After the first day's court appearance, it was the turn of Martin Stephens, Matthew Norman, Si Yi Chen and Tan Duc Thanh Nguyen to go before the judges. Their lawyers had no doubt they were fighting for the lives of their clients, Stephens's lawyer, Adnan Wirawan claiming the prosecution's documents were incomplete and careless.

Scott Rush, Andrew Chan and Renae Lawrence sat through the opening hearings of their cases, with prosecutors outlining the same story of the arrests. Lawrence was the last of the Bali Nine to be brought to court a few days after the mass trials had opened. Wearing a black suit and a white shirt she showed no emotions as she heard through a translator that she was being accused of helping to organise the smuggling attempt before flying to Bali.

She also learned that the gang were being charged individually, which meant, according to her lawyer, she and the others were going to be 'victimised'. But it was suggested to her that she stood a chance of being regarded as a 'victim' if she agreed to testify against other members of the group. For a start, she was reminded, the court had to know that she only took part in the smuggling attempt because Sukumaran and Chan had threatened to kill their families.

The Prosecutor, I Wayan Nastra, added to the pressure already on her by describing in detail how she helped prepare the plot. 'She took to Bali the plastic wrapping, tape and bicycle shorts that she and the three other alleged mules would be found wearing packed with heroin [under their loose outer clothing] 11 days later at Bali airport en route back to Sydney,' he said.

He added that Lawrence 'had no intention of backing out of the operation; the only reason she did not get on the plane was because customs officers stopped her.'

What lay ahead for all nine was months of court appearances, with a chilling end before a firing squad if convicted. But Lawrence had reportedly tried to end her life long before that prospect – police revealed that a month after her arrest, in April, she tried to cut her wrist with a broken bottle in what her lawyer, Anggia Browne, said was probably a suicide attempt. Three months after her arrest she had tried to commit suicide again by slashing her wrists in her jail cell. Chief Inspector General I Made Mangku Pastika said she was covered in blood and was saved after being rushed to hospital. 'We don't know where she got [the razor blade] from,' he said. 'Psychological analysis shows that she is emotionally unstable.' In a further incident she was reported to have broken her arm.

Over the following months pleas were made by defence lawyers to prevent their clients from receiving the death sentence. While three of the four Australians arrested at the Melasti Hotel – Nguyen, Norman and Chen – were tried together, with the others going on trial separately, it was expected that the verdicts would be handed down at much the same time.

In her defence, Lawrence insisted she had received threats against her family and Stephens said the same, adding that Chan had showed him photographs of his family and warned they would be killed if he did not do as he was asked and make the flight to Bali. For his part, Rush said it was Chan who had strapped the heroin packs to his body, wearing rubber gloves as he did so to avoid leaving his fingerprints on the plastic.

Chan, in a statement he read to the court said:

> A lot of lies have been said against me, but the true reality is I'm not what people put me out to be. I've never threatened anybody in my life. The outcome I wish of course, and my family, is that you find that you would release me, for I had nothing to participate in this.

Finally, it was time for the verdicts. Despite Lawrence co-operating with police, for which prosecutors asked for a 20-year sentence, she was given life imprisonment, as was Rush on 13 February 2006. The following day, Czugaj and Stephens were given life. The same sentence was handed down to Norman, Chen and Nguyen.

Sukumaran and Chan, singled out by the judges as the ringleaders on 14 February 2006, were not so fortunate. Their sentence: death. Anti-drug campaigners cheered when Judge Arief Supratman told Chan that he deserved no mercy for organising the smuggling. Chan's only reaction was to shrug before being led away. After Sukumaran learned his fate, judges said the two men would have damaged a generation by exporting 8000 hits of heroin. They had both been evasive and had damaged Bali's reputation and for that there were no grounds for leniency.

In the years that followed, appeals by all convicted smugglers were heard and lifetime prison sentences were reduced – although there were scares when, with an initial appeal failing, death was imposed on Chen, Nguyen, Norman and Rush before the sentences were later reduced to jail terms. But for Sukumaran and Chan, a succession of appeals and pleas for clemency had no impact on their fate. They were to be shot.

The two convicted organisers of the drug run lingered on death row for years as their appeals were heard in vain. Sukumaran held classes for other inmates of Kerobokan, teaching them English and computer skills. A skilled painter, he also arranged art classes. As for Chan, he got married. He met Febyanti Herewila when she was visiting another prisoner in April 2015 and the governor agreed that the pair should be allowed to marry. The prison governor even tried to save the lives of both Sukumaran and Chan, describing them as model prisoners.

On 4 March 2015, Sukumaran and Chan were led from their cells under tight security, handcuffed, and escorted onto a plane by heavily-armed and masked riot-squad police and flown to the port of Cilacap. From there they were taken onto a boat which took them to the prison island of Nusakambangan, also known as 'death island' for it is there that condemned prisoners, such as the Bali bombers and major drug smugglers, are executed.

The two convicted men would have known now that all hope was lost. There were to be nine prisoners who would face the firing squad. Only a miracle could save them.

And we have the extraordinary case of a condemned drug smuggler called Mary Jane Veloso to prove that miracles can happen…

As the days slowly trickled away, it was reported that Myuran Sukumaran felt a 'special connection' to Mary Jane for she was the only woman scheduled to die, although she had been protesting her innocence from the day of her arrest. Sukumaran told others that Mary did not deserve the death penalty. A Filipina maid, she had been arrested coming into Indonesia in April 2010 when 2.6 kilograms of heroin had been found in a suitcase. She claimed she had no idea it was there. All her appeals failed.

In the early hours of 29 April 2015 the jailers came to the isolation cells of Besi prison on Nusakambangan and told the nine condemned prisoners to put on white shirts. It was tragically ironic that there were nine of them: the two Australians, Mary Jane the Filipina, a Brazilian, an Indonesian and four Indonesians, all of them convicted of drug smuggling.

In her isolation cell, Mary Jane clutched a wooden cross and said her prayers as the cell doors were opened. She stood, ready to be led out in the darkness to the convoy of cars waiting to take the prisoners to the place of execution. But then she heard words that came as answers to her prayers: 'You stay here – you are not going to be shot.'

Her life had been spared, thanks to the efforts of a British-born lawyer, Felicity Gerry, who had moved to Australia with her family and had taken up her case. There had also been pleas for mercy, and evidence of her innocence in the Philippines, revealing she had been set up.

As the eight condemned men were being driven to the place of execution, they were reportedly unaware that Mary Jane had not been in the death convoy. But, chillingly, her name had remained on the dashboard of an ambulance that was waiting on the distant docks and due to take her body to a mortuary.

It was shortly after 3 am that the prisoners reached the execution grounds. As they were being led to the posts where they would be tied the group sang *Mighty to Save*. They also sang *Amazing Grace* and *Bless the Lord*. Sydney's *Daily Telegraph* reported the words of a female church minister, Reverend Christie Buckingham, who was allowed to be present at the scene because she was Sukumaran's spiritual adviser. Along with religious advisers for the others, she spent three minutes with Sukumaran after he had been tied to the pole, revealing later that there was a smile on his face as he prayed for those about to shoot him and asked forgiveness for Indonesia.

She said that Sukumaran, and likely the others, had no idea that Mary Jane was not tied up alongside them and that she had been given a reprieve at the last minute. Sukumaran had even prayed for her, asking that she would not be frightened and that she would find peace in God.

The end came, said Reverend Buckingham, when the firing squads took up position and used laser pointers to pinpoint the areas on the chests of the condemned men where the bullets were to strike.

Shots rang out. Then there was silence. It was 12.35 am local time.

Those of the Bali Nine who had been left behind heard the news with shock and despair. But they knew that one day, with reductions in their sentences, they, unlike Myuran Sukumaran and Andrew Chan, would all be able to go home.

CHAPTER TWENTY-FOUR

THE PERILS OF BINTANG

Freedom is a long time coming in Kerobokan.

Even if the sentence is little more than a few years, time drags by in steamy, intolerable surroundings. The gates swing open and closed as the addicts, the pushers, the traffickers, the killers, come and go, some for life, others for much less. But it's hell either way.

One former prisoner, tall, slim English mother Rachel Dougall, who was arrested after being pointed out by British grandmother Lindsay Sandiford and was jailed for 12 months for failing to report a crime, returned home to Britain in 2013, where the 40-year-old told a story of beatings, being locked in a cell with 14 other inmates and suffering a nervous breakdown.

The charge against her of failing to report a crime was related to police allegedly finding small amount of cocaine in a cigarette box at her Bali home. Her long-time partner, antique dealer Julian Ponder, who shared the luxury villa with her and young daughter Kitty and had been sentenced to six years, was left behind when she flew out of Bali.

On her return to Britain she appeared to be making up for the lost 12 months she had spent in Kerobokan when she was seen relaxing on a yacht in Brighton marina. But the memories of prison still clung to her, when she told the *Daily Mail* of being kicked and punched by a large woman prisoner, the start of several savage beatings. Her cellmates included sexually aggressive lesbians, HIV-positive women and drug addicts.

But it was what she had to say about Lindsay Sandiford, sitting out the years on death row, that raised eyebrows. For she claimed that rather than being an unfortunate mule in a drug smuggling operation she was actually the mastermind.

It had been thought that Julian Ponder was the brains behind the plot that allegedly involved a British 'gang of four', made up of Englishman Paul Beales, Ponder, Rachel Dougall and Lindsay Sandiford. The three other members of the group claimed that Lindsay Sandiford had set them up.

'She's not the innocent she would like people to believe,' Rachel claimed on her return to the UK. 'Everyone thinks she's this poor naive granny, but she's not. She doesn't deserve any sympathy.'

Rachel told the *Mail* that Lindsay was 'pure evil,' adding that her excuse of being coerced to carry drugs because her family had been threatened was rubbish, 'She's not some tragic pawn doing it under duress. She blames me for her downfall and says she will have me killed.'

Lindsay has not publicly commented on Rachel's claims, instead keeping the world informed through supporters about how she continued to live in hope of avoiding the firing squad, despite all her appeals being denied.

And while the grandmother and hundreds more are behind bars because of drugs, there are more people walking free but who blame their troubles on the beer. Bintang beer, that is; the staple social 'diet' of locals and tourists. Fights, thefts, injuries and very bad headaches. Poor Bintang, a legacy of Dutch colonial rule, was said to be behind all the woes. Brewed in Indonesia under licence from Heineken, it tastes like Heineken, its green bottle with the red star is similar to that of Heineken, and it's as popular among beer judges as Heineken. In fact, it won a gold medal for Lager (class 2) and Champion Beer in the lager category at the Brewing Industry International Awards in London in 2011.

The company receives plenty of free advertising, possibly more so than any other ale in the world, for Bintang vests are worn everywhere around the island by young and old and there's hardly a table in any bar or restaurant that doesn't have a bottle of the gold-coloured brew. There is also the international promotion, with Bintang vests, bags, bottle holders and T-shirts being seen in the cities of the world in the possession of homeward-bound tourists.

A Singaporean visiting Bali later wrote a blog in which he accused – tongue in cheek – Bintang (4.7 per cent alcohol) for a foolish decision to go climbing. Charles Fulkerson recalled:

> A couple of weeks ago I was on Kuta Beach in Bali with a guy named Mark from Texas and a new friend, Kju, from England. We were drinking beer and watching the sunset when we decided that it would be a good idea to climb

the volcano known as Mt Agung that night (did I mention that we were drinking beer?). Blame it on the Bintang – or our egos – but we decided to opt-out on getting a guide, which all the travel books strong recommended. We arrived at the base at 10.30 pm with just two litres of water each and two 10-packs of Oreo cookies.

Fuelled by the Bintang, the three tourists set off up the mountain and ran into all kinds of troubles, including being set upon by dozens of stray dogs. It took the group eight hours to get to the top and another eight to get down the following day.

Some 50 million litres of the ale are sold in Indonesian each year and there is always a tourist somewhere who will give advice on how many bottles it's safe to drink before a guaranteed morning hangover sets in. One American tourist had a different kind of advice, pointing out how he and his wife survived under 'the scorching sun of Bali'.

> Always order a *large* Bintang beer. It's as much as two small ones and it will cost thirty per cent less. You know you're going to have at least two, anyone, right? If you don't know that now, just wait till you get here and realise the average temperature is somewhere between soaking in sweat and heat stroke.

So, what's in it? The not-so-secret recipe is made up of barley malt from Europe and Australia, hops from Britain and Australia, yeast from Holland and water from a secret Indonesian well (so there is actually one secret ingredient!).

It would require someone with a bag over their head and plugs in their ears to return home from a visit to Bali and not have heard or seen the word Bintang. It rears up constantly in travel websites about the holiday island. A few thoughts from one travel forum:

'Bali is an incredibly beautiful island, with a rich cultural history. But it is a bit difficult to appreciate all that if you are wearing a Bintang singlet and falling down drunk in Kuta.'

Or, 'Buy a Bintang singlet so everyone can see what a cultured bogan you are.'

Or, 'I ventured into Kuta and couldn't get out fast enough. So many

Aussies getting around with tribal tatts and Bintang singlets…really horrible place I thought.'

But there are millions more from around the world who do love Kuta and Bali and that golden nectar called Bintang.

• • •

Late afternoon on the beach. Wives who have offered massage services on the Legian end of Kuta Beach sit in the shade of trees discussing the successes and failures of the day. The sellers of kites of all shapes and sizes, including flying galleons, head back to the road, aware that there won't be any more sales at this time of the day.

Someone has gone to jail today. A rider has fallen off a motorbike. A tourist has been ripped off. A sunbather who has been out too long has turned raw-red. The cell doors are locked in Kerobokan.

As the sun drops lower, young men play a serious barefoot game of soccer, oblivious to the tourists who try to walk past their makeshift playing area. Cameras are raised as vacationers try to catch that last glimpse of sunset, many taking selfies under the brilliant red sky. The dogs have gone home. The mood is changing. Soon the restaurants, bars and nightclubs will come to life as day turns to night.

It's what happens in Bali.

There are no signs that things will be any different tomorrow.

Author photo © Andrew Chant

ABOUT THE AUTHOR

As a career journalist, Richard Shears has covered stories all over the world, from Yellowknife in Canada, to the African continent, the tiny island of Mog Mog in the Pacific and the Antarctic circle. There have been vast oceans and jungles in between. His assignments, one of which has resulted in being awarded a prestigious UK Press award for foreign reporting, have included wars all over the world, among them the conflicts in Iraq, Afghanistan and East Timor. Photos he has taken have been used in magazines and exhibitions. The thirty or so books he has published encompass fiction, true crime and general nonfiction including *Highway to Nowhere: The Chilling True Story of the Backpacker Murders* (1996), *Bloodstain: The Hunt for the Killer of Peter Falconio* (2005), and *Swamp: Who Murdered Margaret Clement?* (2017) for New Holland Publishers.

First published in 2017 by New Holland Publishers

London • Sydney • Auckland

The Chandlery, 50 Westminster Bridge Road, London SE1 7QY, United Kingdom

1/66 Gibbes Street, Chatswood, NSW, 2067, Australia

5/39 Woodside Ave, Northcote, Auckland, 0627, New Zealand

newhollandpublishers.com

Copyright © 2017 New Holland Publishers

Copyright © 2017 in text: Richard Shears

All rights reserved. No part of this publication may be reproduced, stored in a retrieval system or transmitted, in any form or by any means, electronic, mechanical, photocopying, recording or otherwise, without the prior written permission of the publishers and copyright holders.
A record of this book is held at the British Library and the National Library of Australia.

ISBN 9781921024627

Group Managing Director: Fiona Schultz

Publisher: Alan Whiticker

Project Editor: Liz Hardy

Designer: Andrew Davies

Production Director: James Mills-Hicks

10 9 8 7 6 5 4 3 2 1

Keep up with New Holland Publishers on Facebook

facebook.com/NewHollandPublishers

www.ingramcontent.com/pod-product-compliance
Lightning Source LLC
Chambersburg PA
CBHW080638170426
43200CB00015B/2879